BIG [illegible]!

MODERN SIGHTINGS OF FLYING MONSTERS

KEN GERHARD

Illustrations by Bill Rebsamen

Edited and typeset by Jonathan Downes,
Cover design and Layout by Mark North for CFZ Communications
Using Microsoft Word 2000, Microsoft , Publisher 2000, Adobe Photoshop CS.

Cover and Interior illustrations by Bill Rebsamen © 2007

First published in Great Britain by CFZ Press

CFZ Press
Myrtle Cottage
Woolsery
Bideford
North Devon
EX39 5QR

ISBN: 978-1-905723-08-9

- Contents -

FOREWORD

By Jonathan Downes
(Director, Centre for Fortean Zoology)

I have been interested in cryptozoology for about forty years now, and have been working professionally at it since about 1990. Of the main groups of mystery animals, one of the most shamefully neglected are the flying monsters; `things with wings`, as Janet and Colin Bord once described them.

It was a flying monster, which provided me with the first big challenge of my cryptozoological career. I spent some years on the track of a zooform entity known as `The Owlman of Mawnan`; a grotesque flying `thing` that terrorised girls and young women in the vicinity of Mawnan Old Church in southern Cornwall.

It soon became obvious that the owlman was too fantastic a beast to be a *bona fide* flesh and blood animal. It was too strange, too weird, and furthermore it had been reported in a part of the world where the chances of a large, unknown species of flying animal were – realistically – very low indeed.

However, during my researches, I quickly discovered that the owlman was only one of a whole host of giant winged creatures that had been reported across the globe. In 1932-3 – for example - the Percy Sladen Expedition went to West Africa. In charge of the team was Ivan T. Sanderson, a well-known cryptozoologist and writer. While in the Assumbo Mountains in the Cameroons, they made camp in a wooded valley near a steep banked river. They were out hunting near the river when Sanderson shot a large fruit-eating bat. It fell in the water, and as Sanderson was carefully making his way in the fast moving current, he lost his balance and fell. He regained his balance when his companion suddenly shouted *"Look out!"*

"And I looked. Then I let out a shout also and instantly bobbed down under the water, because, coming straight at me only a few feet above the water was a black thing the size of an eagle. I had only a glimpse of its face, yet that was quite sufficient, for its lower jaw hung open and bore a semicircle of pointed white teeth set about their own width apart from each other. When I emerged, it was gone. George was facing the other way blazing off his second barrel. I arrived dripping on my rock and we looked at each other. "Will it come back?" we chorused. And just before it became too dark to see, it came again, hurtling back down the river, its teeth chattering, the air "shss-shssing" as it was cleft by the great, black, dracula-like wings. We were both off-guard, my gun was unloaded, and the brute made straight for George. He ducked. The animal soared over him and was at once swallowed up in the night."

Bernard Heuvelmans – "The Father of Cryptozoology", reprinted this story in his seminal 1958 work, *On the Track of Unknown Animals.* However, Sanderson's original account had also been an inspiration to the man who was my greatest hero; the conservationist and zookeeper Gerald Durrell (1925-95). He even spent time on two of his West African expeditions in 1949 and 1957 trying to find the beast. Well, I thought, if both Durrell and Heuvelmans take such accounts seriously, then there *must* be something in it.

I can't remember when I first heard of the North American `Big Birds`, but it must have been in the late 1980s. The stories fascinated me, and I wished dearly that someone could write a book specifically about them.

In 2004 I was in America making a pilot for a TV series for *Discovery*. Although the series was never made, and I never got paid, the trip was by no means a failure. One night, after I had spent the day interviewing witnesses to a strange, blue, dog-like creature outside San Antonio in Texas, I met up with Texan cryptozoologist, and musician Ken Gerhard, and his lovely wife Lori.

It soon became obvious that we had a heck of a lot in common, and by the end of the evening we were firm friends. We spent hours talking about our various projects, and promised that we would collaborate on various ventures in the future. It was only at the end of the evening when Ken – almost as an afterthought – told me that he was planning to write a book about the `Big Bird` reports. Was he, I asked diffidently, looking for a publisher? It turned out that he was, and so, one balmy November night in San Antonio, only a stone's throw from The Alamo, with the sounds of crickets, tree frogs, and the trickle of running water from the hotel's ornamental fountain, in the air, the deal was done.

Just over two years later, I find myself sitting in my study in rural North Devon, reliving the memories of that night. Ken, old friend: It is a true honour to be able to write an introduction to such a remarkable book.

Jonathan Downes,
The Centre for Fortean Zoology
Woolfardisworthy,
North Devon.
January 2007

PROLOGUE

I hunt monsters.

For nearly a quarter of a century, when the opportunity has arisen, I have investigated reports of bizarre, incomprehensible creatures throughout North America, and other parts of the world. The evidence that has been collected by my fellow cryptozoologists who research such matters, seems to indicate that some monsters are not merely legends. Rather, they may in fact be actual, living, entities that occupy the outer reaches.

Many of our brightest investigators have concluded that our monsters may be rarely seen, as yet undiscovered or presumably extinct animals. We know from the fossil record that giant reptiles once occupied the oceans, and the land was once occupied by pre-human ape-men. So, is it simply a coincidence that there are thousands of documented accounts of reptilian sea serpents? And an equal number of reports of hairy, wildmen? These reports have been prevalent throughout man's recorded history and continuing into modern times.

What about reports of monsters that fly?

During the autumn of 2003, I became aware of a weird, winged beast that had been spotted mere miles from my home in Texas, and I was instantly swept into an investigation that would take me south to the Mexican border. Three decades earlier, Texas' Rio Grande Valley had been the sight of well-publicised events that revolved around a nightmarish creature. The mysterious animal was usually described as being charcoal black and as tall as a man, with bat-like wings and large, red eyes. Some described its "horrible" face as looking like a monkey, cat or bat, while others recalled its long, pointed beak. Most impressive was the creature's huge wingspan, which was reported to be anywhere from twelve to over twenty feet across. The local media, playing upon the popularity of a character from the children's television program *Sesame Street,* named the monster `Big Bird`.

While the Big Bird mystery remains unsolved, it is worth noting that there are no recognised birds, either native to Texas, or indeed anywhere else, that can claim a twenty-foot wingspan. There were, however, such creatures in the distant past. Animals that resembled flying dragons ruled the skies for nearly two hundred million years, before supposedly disappearing into extinction. Some were as large as aeroplanes.

But are they really extinct? In my first book *Monsters are Real,* I refuted the position that there are no other holdovers from our prehistoric past. How can our scientists be so sure that they have accounted for Earth's major animal species, when new discoveries are still being made all the time?

One fine example is the gigantic, man-eating species of lizard known as the Komodo dragon, (*Varanus komodoensis*) discovered on an Indonesian island less than a century ago. Prior to its discovery, the Komodo dragon was considered to be a legend by westerners, although natives on nearby islands were uncomfortably familiar with the creature; The Sultan of Sumbawa – a neighbouring island, used the island of Komodo as a penal colony, and even encouraged these huge lizards to execute criminals.

Much more recently, scientists verified the jungle-dwelling Vu Quang ox (*Pseudoryx nghetinhensis*) of northern Vietnam during July of 1992, when a skull and hide were produced for the very first time. During 1994, the giant muntjac, (*Muntiacus vuquangensis*) a previously unknown type of deer was also discovered in the Vu Quong forests. The following year, a herd of prehistoric horses were discovered living in a remote, Tibetan valley. The Riwoche horses had been cut off from the outside world for thousands of years and were presumed to be long extinct. Many readers are probably already familiar with the story of the rediscovered coelacanth fish, *(Latimeria chalumnae)* rediscovered in 1938, as well as the giant squid (**Architeuthidae** family) – an enormous animal about which practically nothing is known.

The giant muntjac was discovered in Vietnam as recently as 1994

New bird species are still being documented as well. Several new birds have been found in the dense, mountain forests and jungles of South America during the past decade. Even in the southern United States, there are indications that the great ivory-billed woodpecker (*Campephilus principalis*) is still alive and well, despite being considered extinct for seventy years.

Perhaps marine Biologist Phillippe Bouchet put it best in the May of 2006, after discovering a new species of crustacean that had been considered extinct for sixty million years. *"There are places on this planet incredibly remote and little explored,"* According to the Associated Press, on May 19th, Bouchet told one reporter, *"In the first years of the 21st century, the exploration of planet Earth is not over"* Indeed, there do remain many remote areas of our planet where few men, if any have ever set foot and those areas are vast.

So read on and decide for yourself, as I present the evidence for flying monsters in a modern world. Irregardless of your final conclusion, I predict one thing for certain:

...you will be watching the skies as never before.

Chapter 1

- Impossible Encounters -

On a humid autumn day in 2003, I was seeking refuge from Houston's heat in my heavily air-conditioned house when the phone rang. The caller was a friend of mine, with whom I'd made several trips into Texas' Big Thicket, [1] searching for the legendary giant known as Big-foot. Now he was really busting to tell me something. *"You're not going to believe what this guy at work told me he saw,"* my caller excitedly blurted. Having had a long time interest in various paranormal phenomena, I took his statement as a sort of challenge, since I am always fairly open-minded to any potential absurdity that looms ahead. My associate, who goes by the colourful nickname `Bam Bamm`, went on to explain how his co-worker had been hesitant to tell the story, due to heavy ridicule he had endured in the past. Apparently, our extreme interest in a fringe sub-ject like Bigfoot had given this fellow the courage to confide in somebody once again.

At the time, both men were working as contract electricians on the city's massive new rail sys-tem, and were shooting the breeze as they travelled together in a company truck. During a break in the dialogue, the co-worker had softly confessed, *"I don't know anything about Bigfoot, but when I was younger I saw a leathery bird or pterodactyl, like on the Flintstones (cartoon show)."* The implication of the statement struck me at once, as others have made fabulous claims of winged reptiles in modern times, particularly in parts of south Texas. Bam Bamm went on to ex-plain to me that he had made this witness draw a sketch of what he had seen and that the animal definitely appeared to be prehistoric in nature. He concluded the call by saying that he felt his workmate was being sincere, and did not seem to be the joking type. Intrigued, I requested that both men pay me a visit as soon as possible so that I might be able to hear the account first hand. A couple of days later, they stopped by my home after getting off work.

The eyewitnesses' name was Richard Guzman. He was a somewhat short, stocky, middle aged Hispanic man with a moustache, and a soft spoken voice. I deduced by his calloused handshake that he had been no stranger to hard work. Richard began by explaining, as Bam Bamm had pre-viously, that whenever he had told anybody about his sighting, he was inevitably accused of hav-ing indulged in drugs or alcohol. Basically, he was ridiculed. This is unfortunately a very com-mon reaction when people who witness unexplained phenomena confide in others. It is undenia-bly the main reason that the majority of these remarkable encounters never come to light.

Richard next informed me that there was another witness to the incident; his best friend Rudy. Unfortunately, Rudy's life had taken a turn for the worse and he was currently incarcerated in the Houston City Jail.

According to Richard, both men were in their early twenties at the time, though he is not sure of the exact date or year. He thought it was probably around 1983, but admitted that it could have been a year or two earlier. He recalled that it was a hot and clear day at around six in the evening. The two, young men were talking, and leaning on Guzman's Chrysler, which was parked in front of his family's house on Lucore Street in southeast Houston. Suddenly, they both caught sight of a strange animal that was flying about fifty feet off the ground, around forty yards away. They both watched it for about fifteen seconds, as it flapped its wings a couple of times and then glided out of sight into some tall trees to the southeast. Immediately, the two young men locked eyes in startled disbelief and began to question each other, in order to confirm that they had both seen the same thing… they apparently had.

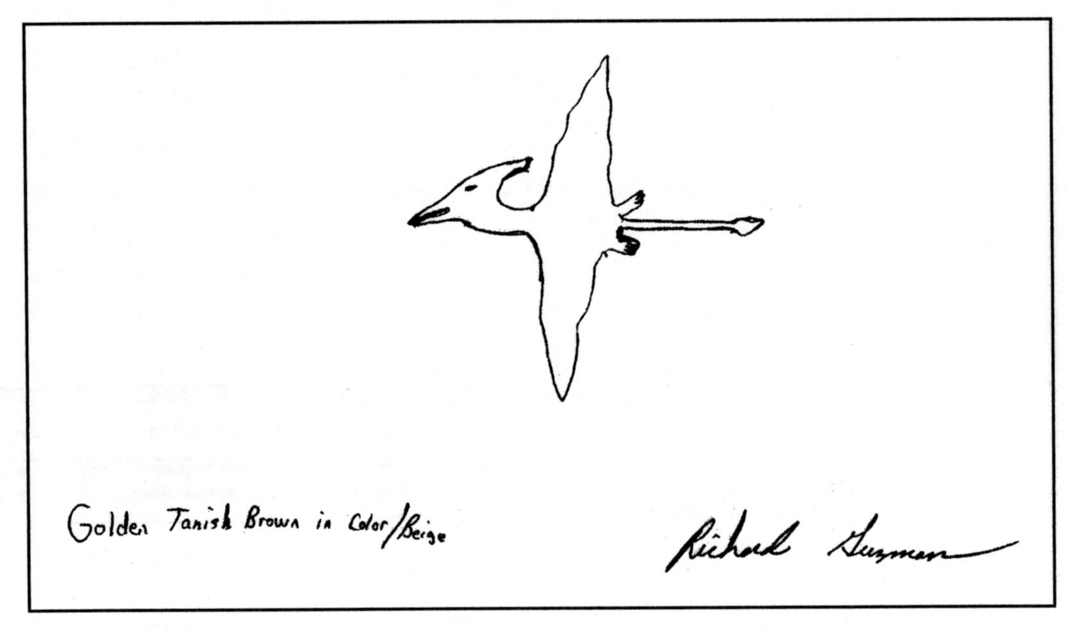

This is the third sketch drawn by eyewitness Richard Guzman

Richard continued, *"What first got me was the head and tail."* He explained that the first thing he'd noticed was a prominent hump on the back of the creature's head, and even *more* noticeable; a two-foot, snakelike tail that terminated in a fin. Guzman described the animal's entire five-foot long body and bat-like wings as appearing featherless, and resembling brown - or beige - leather. Though he did not clearly remember if any legs or other appendages were sticking out, Richard did recall one other fleeting detail. There appeared to be some sort of noticeable indentation in the side of the creature's skull. He finished up by informing me that Rudy would back up his story one hundred percent, if - and when - I could obtain a separate interview with him.

I was, of course, mesmerized by this account. I next asked Guzman to sketch what he had seen as Bam Bamm had, in order to confirm what he was describing; essentially an animal that had been presumed to be extinct for millions of years. About a week later, Richard submitted a third drawing to me on his own initiative. All three sketches, which were made days apart, are virtually identical. At the conclusion of Richard's interview, I had explained to him how other people in modern day Texas had reported similar encounters with flying reptiles known as pterosaurs. To prove my point, I grabbed my copy of the book, *In Search of Prehistoric Survivors* by Dr Karl Shuker, and began to read from a section that was titled `Pterosaurs in Texas?` Soon we were all enthralled, as I read aloud the account given by ambulance driver James Thompson of Harlingen.

"His tail is what caught my attention," Thompson had stated. This was almost verbatim what Guzman had expressed to me a few minutes earlier. The book went on to explain how on the afternoon of September 14th 1983, Thompson had been returning from a routine inspection on nearby South Padre Island. He was travelling west on Highway 100, roughly four miles to the east of Los Fresnos, when suddenly he caught sight of a strange, flying animal about a hundred and fifty feet ahead of him. Thompson later stated, *"I saw him fly right in front of me. I was the only one who stopped because he flew right in front of me. I guess nobody else saw him. I expected him to land like a model aeroplane. That's what I thought he was, but he flapped his wings enough to get above the grass."*

James Thompson's description sounded eerily familiar. He had estimated the creature's wingspan to *be "At least the width of the ambulance,"* which was five or six feet across and that its total length appeared to be about eight to ten feet, including the tail. *"It had a black, or greyish rough*

The location where Richard Guzman sighted an unusual flying animal.

texture. It wasn't feathers. I'm quite sure it was a hide type covering," Thompson had insisted. He had remembered that its very thin tail which had caught his attention at first, ended in a sort of fin. Apparently, he had driven up on the animal so fast, that the tail almost hit his ambulance. Thompson had also noticed that on the back of the creature's head, there appeared to be a hump, like that of a Brahma bull, and that it also had a kind of pouch beneath its short neck that resembled, *"something like a pelican's pouch."* Thompson had actually pulled over on the side of the road and gotten out of his vehicle to get a better view, as the weird apparition glided out of sight.

"I just watched him fly away," he recalled. After looking through some science books, James Thompson later declared the animal he saw to be a pterodactyl.

Considering the timeframe and proximity of these two sightings, there may be a connection. Both Guzman and Thompson claimed to have seen an unusual flying animal during the early 1980s in southeast Texas. They both described a creature which scientists claim has not existed for sixty-five million years.

Half a world away in Africa, there is another well-documented encounter that may have some relevance, as well.

The sighting took place during January of 1956, in the nation of Northern Rhodesia (now Zaire), specifically on a road just northwest of Lake Bangweulu. (2) A thirsty engineer named J.P.F. Brown had pulled over his Land Rover, in order to retrieve the flask that he kept in his boot. Suddenly, according to the witness, two strange, prehistoric-looking birds flew silently overhead and out of sight. Brown later noted that both creatures possessed extremely long tails. In addition, he had observed that their dog-like heads appeared narrow, with muzzle-like jaws and sharp, little teeth. Brown estimated that the animals were about four and a half feet long, with three and a half foot wingspans.

The location where James Thompson had his sighting in 1983

The field where James Thompson last watched his "mystery bird."

A comparison of all three reports is quite compelling when we consider that anatomically speaking, there are no currently recognized animals that adequately fit these descriptions. In particular, no winged animals possess a long, serpentine tail with a diamond shape on the end. Instead, we must look into the distant past, over a hundred and forty million years ago. During the Jurassic Era, there were flying reptiles that match all of these descriptions perfectly. They were the early group of pterosaurs known as the rhamphorhynchoids.

Chapter 2
- 1976 -

The Bicentennial year began with high weirdness in the Rio Grande Valley of Texas. In Cameron County, where James Thompson would claim a pterosaur sighting eight years later, a series of encounters with a winged monster named `Big Bird` would soon make international headlines. The first rumours of strange, flying beasts actually started the previous October in a place called Robstown, which lies up the coast near Corpus Christi. One notable sighting was rumoured to have taken place from a school playground. Those rumours quickly spawned some humorous editorials about the monster sightings in the Corpus Christi newspaper. Others spoofs about the reports ran on a local television station. The winged, mystery creature was generally described as being large and black with red markings on its back.

Around that same time period, rumours of a half-human/half-bird were also trickling out of Rio Grande City in Starr County to the west. Locals in that town whispered that the man-bird could be seen some nights perched on the roof of a local tavern, while other times it lurked on the roof of the county court house. By the end of November, the flying thing reports had polarized in Cameron County. First, a terrified San Benito man rushed into the local police station and stated that he had just seen the monster bird. *"I'm not drunk. I'm sober. But I saw it,"* he told the officers on duty. Soon after that incident, two kids also stopped by the station to also report a large bird, adding that the animal had a bald head like a monkey.

The first widely publicised sighting happened on New Year's Day of 1976. Eleven year old Tracey Lawson and fourteen year old Jackie Davies were at Tracey's house, which faced a ploughed field on Ed Carey road in south Harlingen. Incidentally, this location lies only a few miles northwest of James Thompson's encounter and is also close to the Colorado Arroyo River. As the two girls played in the back yard, they suddenly noticed a horrifying animal standing next to an irrigation canal about a hundred yards away. It appeared to be a five-foot, black bird with wide, bunched-up wings, a "gorilla-like" face, and a thick, six-inch beak. After running into the house and grabbing a pair of binoculars, the cousins could see that the creature was watching them with large, menacing, red eyes. At one point, the thing even let out an eerie, high-pitched screech. Eventually, the animal appeared to vanish, only to reappear a few minutes later on the northeast corner of the property, where it seemed to be peering at the two girls from behind the bushes. This apparently was the final straw that sent Jackie and Tracy racing inside to wake Tracey's parents. Either unconvinced by the children's story, or perhaps feeling the excesses of the previous evening's celebration, the parents refused to go outside and investigate at the time.

However, the next day, Jackie's stepfather Tom Waldon decided to have a look around, and discovered some remarkable three-toed tracks where the `thing` had apparently been standing. The first three tracks were near a fence right behind the house, with a fourth impression twenty yards away, and a fifth print lying twenty yards beyond that. The tracks were squared at the head, with a well-rounded impression in the back. They measured a whopping twelve inches long by eight inches across, as well as sinking an inch and a half deep into the ground. Tom excitedly called his

The Colorado Arroyo River, near Ed Carey Road in Harlingen

wife at work. Soon after, she alerted Tracey's father Stan, along with the local sheriff's office. When all parties had gathered at the location a little while later, one hundred and seventy pound (12 st.) Stan attempted to set his own footprint in the ground, and was unable to make an indentation that was anywhere near as deep as those found by Tom. Word of these strange events quickly reached Harlingen television station KGBT, who sent out a camera crew to film the strange goings-on. When the story ran on the evening news the following night, it created a quiet buzz around the valley.

Stan Lawson soon recalled other unusual events from that evening. He remembered how his dog had cowered in its kennel, not wanting to come out and eat. At one point, the dog had even bolted in the house, and had to be dragged outside. Also, there had been the sound of something scraping against one of the windows. The next morning, Stan had found the outside screen torn, though he couldn't remember if it had been a pre-existing condition. Also, their neighbour, Sgt. Sam Esparza of the San Benito police had stopped by to mention how he had found bloodstains on two sheets that he had hung out to dry that same evening. It was as if, in his opinion, something had vomited half-digested liver down the white sheets. According to his wife, Sgt. Esparza's Doberman had also cowered inside his house all night for no apparent reason.

The next well-publicised sighting occurred during the early morning hours of January 3rd, when two San Benito police officers reported seeing a huge bird swooping over their separate patrol cars. The creature that the officers watched, possessed a long neck that was curled up into an S shape as it flew. Officers Arturo Padilla and Homero Galvan would soon have an explanation.

The two men had simply seen a large pelican, according to a local wildlife expert. Padilla had in fact stated that, *"It more or less looked like a stork or pelican type of bird. The wingspan, I guess, was about like a pretty good sized car, about fifteen feet or so. The colour was white. I've done a lot of hunting, but I've never seen anything like it. The thing was really oversized."* Indeed, because as we will discover later, a pelican with a fifteen foot wingspan *would* be an undocumented monster.

A frightening encounter occurred five nights later, on Wednesday, January 7th at around 8:30pm. Alverico Guajardo was eating dinner in his trailer home, just outside of Brownsville, when suddenly there was a loud thud, as if a large bag of sand or concrete had struck the outside wall. Fearing for his family's safety, Guajardo grabbed a knife, and stuck it in his pocket, before venturing out into the darkness. He could only make out the silhouette of a large animal lying on the ground. Because he had no flashlight on hand, Alverico went to his station wagon, and switched on the headlights. This action caused the thing to rise, and Guajardo could see that it was a brown, winged, creature standing about four feet tall. He would later state, *"I was scared. It's got wings like a bird, but it's not a bird. That animal is not from this world."*

Alverico described the animal as having silver dollar sized *"terrible-looking eyes"*, a three to four-foot beak, and large wings that covered most of its body. As the two beings stared at each other at a distance of fifteen feet for about two minutes, the creature made a "terrible" pulsing noise which seemed to emanate from its throat. At no time did Guajardo see its beak move. Curiously though, the animal did not fly away, but rather chose to back slowly into the darkness, until it could no longer be seen. Alverico seemed genuinely terrified by his encounter, according to reporter George Cox of the *Brownsville Herald*, who interviewed him the next morning. *"I'd say he saw something,"* Cox later remarked.

When Guajardo's story made the Herald's front page the following day, it began a virtual whirlwind. As a publicity stunt, radio station KRIO in nearby McAllen offered up a thousand dollar reward for the `Big Bird`. To complicate matters, some locals began to consider that there might be a connection to a series of recent livestock mutilations in the area. Texas Parks and Wildlife Commission officer Ed Dutch quickly reacted to the bounty, by issuing a statement which read: *"We have a number of species of birds that do exist in South Texas in the Valley area, many of which have wingspans up to perhaps 10 feet or in excess of 10 feet, and some of them are on the rare endangered species list. All birds are protected by state or federal law, so if any of these birds should be killed or chased or caught for whatever reason it may be they're going to be subject to prosecution by state or federal officials."* [3]

The livestock mutilations had actually started two months earlier, when Bayview rancher John Berrera found two of his cows dead. Both of the animal's hearts, sex organs, rectums, tongues and tails had been surgically removed. Another dead cow was discovered by Berrera within a week. It possessed similar wounds to the first two. Raymondville resident Joe Suarez found one of his goats mutilated a few weeks later, on the evening of December 25th. In that case, the animal's heart and lungs were missing, as well as its snout. Joe's goat was found lying in a pool of warm blood, with no tracks around its carcass. Shortly thereafter, a Los Fresnos man named Mack Miller reported that one of his young calves had been found dead, with its tongue and one eye missing. Captain Donald Duncan of the sheriff's office released a statement that the county had been experiencing increased cattle deaths since early November and that they appeared to be from natural causes, adding that many animals showed no signs of mutilation.

Subsequently, my own investigations led to an e-mail from a Mari M. who wrote, "The Big Bird story had connotations of men in black and government conspiracies... my aunt and uncle did experience something with cow mutilations... my aunt while driving in the back roads of Raymondville and Lyford saw a cow that had its hooves removed and a whole near its rectum... no blood... no tracks... people talked about military helicopters and ufos." It is a fact that on the evening of January 03rd, multiple witnesses in San Benito had reported a U.F.O. that flew east towards Olmito, before disappearing into the Resaca de La Palma canal.

If U.F.O.s or the military were somehow connected to the Big Bird, it would possibly explain why two supply specialists from San Antonio's Kelly Air Force Base were the next to claim a sighting. On the eleventh of January, forty-four year old Jesse Garcia and forty year old Vanacio Rodriguez were at a four hundred acre ranch just north of Poteet. "I was checking out a stock tank," Garcia later explained. "I looked out and saw the bird standing in the water. We were about three hundred feet away from it. It looked about five feet tall. He started flying, but I never saw him flap his wings. He made no noise at all."

As newspapers around Texas and the Valley began to run more stories about the strange visitor, other details came to light. Old timers had been whispering that the bird had actually been around the area for a long time. Some even had other names for the Big Bird, such as Lechuza and also Tacuache, which apparently means possum is Spanish. Reporter Mike Hess of the San Antonio Express News wrote that Tacuache was, "The offspring of an unsolicited union between a vampire bat and a Robstown woman. The beast was first described as having the face of the woman who was raped. Later as it moved farther south the bird fell prey to several descriptions."

At some point, a Brownsville resident named Enrique Pena came forward to tell the police that he saw Big Bird on the ground at close range. Pena described the bird as standing five feet tall and walking very much like a man. Another Brownsville woman reported that she had seen a bird as big as a car near the city port. Residents in the tiny town of Olmito reported sightings of a strange bird that resembled a flying rhea or ostrich.

Meanwhile, radio station KRIO, which was still trying to maximize the promotional value of the whole affair, sent its news director James Moore out to capture Big Bird. After doing some investigation, Moore had concluded that there were in fact two of the animals and that they were nesting near San Benito. "That explains all the people who have seen it," he had reasoned, "There are two of them." According to Moore, he had received tips from listeners which had led him to his conclusions and for the record he stated that, "It's not anything from out of this world, either." The adventurous news director seemed determined to break the story himself and would not divulge much information, other than his intent to capture one of the creatures alive. After receiving a tip about a possible nesting area, Moore was disappointed to find out that the culprits were actually barn owls. Following one secretive Tuesday night expedition, he had confessed, "We still have hopes someone will capture it alive."

The scariest encounter with Big Bird involved a twenty-six year old man named Armando Grimaldo, just north of Raymondville in neighbouring Willacy County. On the evening of January 14th, Grimaldo was smoking a cigarette on his mother-in-law's porch. His estranged wife Cristina

Armando Grimaldo described his attacker as having bat-like wings

was sleeping inside the house at the time. As Armando would later put it, "I heard a sound like the flapping of bat like wings and a funny kind of whistling. The dogs in the neighbourhood started barking. I looked around but I couldn't see nothing. I don't why I never looked up. I guess I should have, but as I was turning to go look over the other side of the house, I felt something grab me, something with big claws. I looked back and saw it and started running. I've never been so scared in my whole life."

Armando described his assailant as having ten to twelve-foot, bat-like wings with dark, leathery, featherless skin, and a monkey-like face with large red eyes. He did not recall seeing a beak on the creature. As he attempted to flee from his attacker, Grimaldo could feel its claws grasping and then tearing his jacket and shirt. In desperation to escape, Armando dove down onto the ground and crawled on his belly until he was under a bushy tree. He thought he could heardthe creature's heavy panting, as it flew off into the night. Within a few minutes, Cristina, as well as his neighbours found him screaming and shaking in the back yard. The victim reportedly was in shock when Cristina called the police a little later. When help arrived on the scene, Grimaldo was repeatedly mumbling the word pajaro, which means bird in Spanish. He was even taken to Willacy County Hospital, where it was determined that he had escaped any real injury. However, Armando did remain bed ridden for two days after the incident.

The sightings seemed to reach a crescendo after Armando Grimaldo's story hit the papers, with reports emanating from as far away as Laredo. In that instance Arturo Rodriguez and his nine year old nephew Ricardo were reportedly fishing on the Rio Grande River, when they noticed a gigantic, grey bird gliding overhead. Arturo wisely took his nephew and fled the scene. Laredo resident named Roberto Gonzalez claimed that he saw the same bird flying over highway 83, within two hours of the Rodriguez sighting.

Back in the lower Valley, two sisters named Libby and Deany Ford were at pond several miles northeast of Brownsville, when they claim they saw Big Bird around mid January. According to both women, the animal that they observed was man-sized and black with bat-like face and wings. After looking through some text books afterward, the sisters agreed that what they had seen closely resembled an extinct pteranodon.

Throughout this period, local newspaper articles about the Big Bird were being picked up by the big news services and distributed throughout the country, as various media outlets began to pluck them off the wire. The notion of a real monster scare in 1976 was fascinating to most. Talk show host Johnny Carson mentioned Big Bird on the *Tonight Show*, joking that it would eventually prove to be aviator Howard Hughes. Tejano recording artists Wally "The Taco Kid" Gonzalez and Raul Ruiz wrote and recorded popular songs about the "Pajaro Grande." The bizarre events even made headlines as far away as Germany, appearing on the front page of the newspaper *Die Bild Zeitung*. Decades later, there is even a Japanese action figure that pays homage to the winged mystery, proving that Big Bird has become a global phenomenon in many respects.

The sightings continued for a little while. On the seventeenth, an unidentified man called the Cameron County sheriff's department to report that his family had spotted a five-foot, cat or monkey-faced bird with a twelve-foot wingspan crossing FM 1575 near Olmito. That same day, San Benito police received a call from residents Homer and Maria Hernandez, who claimed they observed a four-foot bird with a four to six inch beak at an irrigation canal. Also around that time, a large, brown bird was reportedly seen flying over a canal at Raymondville

At the height of Big Bird Mania on January 18th, eccentric Abilene oil man Jack Grimm, who had previously financed expeditions searching for Bigfoot, Loch Ness Monster and Noah's Arc, announced that he was putting up a five thousand dollar reward for the Big Bird's capture. Grimm's only stipulation was that the captured animal would have to be verified as being a new or thought to be extinct species, with a wingspan in excess of fifteen feet. An unidentified Houston woman quickly upped the ante by phoning the San Benito police department and offering an additional reward of five hundred dollars. Perhaps her offer was not taken too seriously though, since the piece of paper with her name and phone number was accidentally thrown away by an employee.

Consequently, a few more reports trickled in, though the precise details were often a bit vague. As the monster's fame began to spread throughout the nation and the world, demand for more news of the bird drove some reporters of south Texas newspapers to produce more articles. Unfortunately, many writers chose to do humorous editorials on the topic, rather than investigating Big Bird as a bona fide mystery animal.

One reporter who stayed hot on the trail was George Cox of the Brownsville Herald. In an interview with the San Antonio News, Cox told reporter Jack McGrath, "Some are really taking this seriously. I met with three men who have a command post set up for the hunt. They even have all the sightings plotted on a big map on the wall." Cox confessed that he may have had a sighting himself. While patrolling with a sheriff's deputy, both he and the officer saw a large bird way off in the distance. "It was pretty far off but it sure looked big," he remarked. Commenting on another report, Cox said, "We have one where the bird ran, jumped and glided across a canal. It hit the ground on the other side and started running again."

On the twenty-second came a bombshell from up the valley in Eagle Pass. A man named Francisco Magallanes Jr. claimed that he was attacked in an incident that mirrored the assault on Armando Grimaldo. The twenty-one year old Magallanes told police that he went into his backyard around 12:45 am to investigate a noise and noticed an unknown creature in a stooped position. According to Francisco, the black, bat-winged animal then rose to a height of six-feet and pounced upon him, scratching him badly in the ensuing struggle. Magallanes somehow managed to break free and run inside his house to safety. Upon further questioning, he revealed other details. Francisco described the creature as having the face of a pig with bright, red eyes and pointy ears, long arms, stubby legs and an eight-foot wingspan. He claimed that the monster made a hissing sound like a snake and when it was touching him, his skin would become hot. A doctor that examined Magallanes concluded that scratches on his shoulder could be authentic, but later, the doctor turned out to be the victim's close friend. After further questioning by police, Francisco also admitted that had been drinking at the time and soon inconsistencies in his story began to appear. As a result, most researchers now view this particular incident with extreme skepticism.

Further up the valley in Del Rio, there were three different reports on January 23rd and 24th. On the 23rd, the Barrera family apparently spotted a dark, stork like-bird. That same day, two other Del Rio residents claimed that they also sighted a big, black bird. The following day, a large, bluish-grey bird was reported by yet another eyewitness.

By the end of January, activity seemed to die down. Though, to the northwest, there was an attempt by the media to manufacture a `Big Bird` story on February 11th. It all started when farm workers two miles south of San Antonio's famous Alamo noticed a great blue heron perched in a fruit orchard. The somewhat rare, three-foot bird appeared to be somewhat disoriented. Within an hour, a crowd of fifty people had gathered to watch the indifferent animal and eventually a TV crew appeared to capture the whole scene. The text that would accompany the highly circulated footage, inferred that this was the `Big Bird` perhaps in its unglamorous demise and a "boring portrayal of a legend."

On Tuesday, February 24th, there was an incident near San Antonio that was anything but boring. The report involved three teachers in the city's Southside School District. Patricia Bryant, Marsha Dahlberg and David Rendon were driving to work in separate cars on an isolated road, when an enormous bird suddenly swooped low over their cars, casting a shadow across the road. When all three teachers pulled over to get a better look, they could see both the first bird, as well as a second animal in the distance. Both animals appeared to be circling above a herd of cattle like gigantic buzzards. Mrs. Bryant later recalled, *"I could see the skeleton of this bird through the skin or feathers or whatever and it stood out black against the background of the grey feathers."*

The location near San Antonio where the three teachers had their sighting

Rendon added, *"It just glided. It didn't fly. It was no higher than the telephone line. It had a huge breast. It had different legs and it had huge wings, but the wings were very peculiar like. It had a bony structure, you know, like when you hold a bat by the wing tips, like it has bones at the top and in between."* Bryant continued, *"It was just enormous and frightening. I told my husband it was as big as a Piper Cub and he just laughed at me. I think the wingspan was 15 or 20 feet if not more."* Like the Ford sisters and later James Thompson, the three teachers attempted to identify the animals they saw by looking through an encyclopaedia. The three teachers came to the conclusion that the two birds had most resembled extinct pteranodons.

Towards the end of 1976, there were similar reports from the Montalba/Bethel area, hundreds of miles to the north near Dallas. It is unclear however, if the animal seen by residents there matches up with the descriptions from the valley. In the most detailed incident, Montalba hog farmer John Carroll Jr. claimed he encountered an eight-foot tall bird standing in his pond one day. Carroll stated that the bird's colour was a bluish steel-grey, with a golden hued breast. In his estimation, it possessed a foot-long bill and a weight that easily exceeded one hundred pounds. He even claimed that he shot at the creature but wasn't sure if he hit it, though he did find a blood stained feather that wasn't readily identified. Irregardless, it had seemed to Carroll that the bird was so big that it was having problems getting airborne. Another eyewitness in the area, Bethel resident Doloris Moore, described a bird she saw standing in her yard as looking, *"very large, like a big crane seen through a magnifying glass."*

In retrospect, the dramatic events of 1976 resulted in other previously unreported encounters with `Big Bird` coming to light, like that of Jesus Martinez of Donna, Texas who claimed a sighting back in 1970. While driving home from the town of Welasco, on Highway 63, one evening, Martinez claimed he spotted a brown bird, which seemed to be as long as his car, possessing what he estimated to be a sixteen-foot wingspan. He stated that its head and beak reminded him of an eagle. Another eyewitness named M. Gonzales remembered seeing an unusual, brown bird near Harlingen around 1971. George Cox had interviewed another man, who claimed he had seen the `Big Bird` a year and a half prior to the events of 1976, but was afraid to come forward for fear of ridicule.

Brownsville resident Alex Resendez, who I met at a `Big Bird` lecture, claims to have had two different sightings in the 1970s, *"I saw the bird twice. One time here in Brownsville and one time by Mission,"* Resendez told reporter Kevin Garcia of the *Brownsville Herald* in a recent newspaper article. On the first occasion, he had apparently overheard a broadcast on his C.B. radio one evening, in which someone was reporting that Big Bird was perched on top of the Brownsville police station. Out of curiosity, Alex decided to go over and take a look for himself. To his amazement, he claims that he actually could see a large, shadowy bird perched on the station's rooftop, although certain attributes seemed to make the creature invisible to the officers below.

Resendez also speaks of a dramatic encounter that he and his family had while living in the country, near the town of Edinburg. According to Alex, he was taking a nap one evening when his young, son began to shout out that `Big Bird` was standing in a nearby cow pasture. Alex went outside to have a look, and sure enough, there was a very large, brown bird with a strange, transparent-looking beak, standing only about fifty yards away. In his excitement, the boy ran and jumped over a fence to get a better view of the creature and was immediately confronted by an angry bull. To everyone's amazement, the bull began to charge at the young boy, but then changed its direction at the last second, and instead raced at the bird, which in turn flew away. According to Alex, he was able to observed blue and white stripes on the undersides of the animal's wings.

Three decades have now passed since that eventful year, and - not surprisingly - `Big Bird` has become a major part of south Texas folklore; particularly in the Rio Grande Valley. So much so, in fact, that virtually everyone I have met from that region knows of someone who has had a personal sighting or experience. Nostalgic articles still appear in the local newspapers too, *especially* around Halloween, when readers are intrigued by spooky topics. Reporter Alma Walzer of the McAllen Monitor penned one such piece in November, 2004. Alma's research revealed a treasure trove of personal `Big Bird` anecdotes that has manifested in the archives of local Pan American University. Students attending there who grew up in the Valley are encouraged to write about their favourite local legends. `Big Bird` is understandably a popular choice. One student named Esequiel from the town of Pharr just outside of McAllen, wrote of a sighting he had when he was in the sixth grade. He remembered that he and one of his friends watched an enormous bird-like object in the sky one day. Another Pan American student named Yadira wrote about how he had heard of a man from Olmito, who claimed he was attacked by `Big Bird` while leaving a bar one night. The man's wife had supposedly accused him of making up the whole story, until she discovered some feathers on the floorboard of their car the following morning.

In retrospect, the events of 1976 will always be remembered as part of a bigger monster craze that seemed to circumvent the globe during the late 1970s. [4] We can probably chalk at least a few of the `Big Bird` accounts up to imaginative storytelling or perhaps confusion, inspired by the fervour of the period. But, if we are to believe that observers of the unknown such as eyewitness Richard Guzman often suppress their experiences for fear of ridicule, then there may be dozens, if not hundreds of other eyewitnesses who have decided not to go on the record. It is my sincere hope that these individuals will find the strength to come forward and add their testimony to the growing body of evidence.

Chapter 3

- Journey to the Outer Edge -

Two years after the weird events of 1976 had transpired, a book titled *Creatures from the Outer Edge* was published. It was written by Jerome Clark, a paranormal author and a budding cryptozoologist named Loren Coleman. In their book, the two authors discuss numerous reports of unexplained creatures that were documented during the paranormally active 1970s. For a chapter titled *Things with Wings*, Clark had even travelled to south Texas during the March of 1976, in order to investigate the `Big Bird` while the trail was still relatively warm. Consequently, the intrepid researcher was successful in bringing many, important new details to light.

For example, we now know of a possible sighting by an associate of former Corpus Christi newspaper editor James Rowe. The eyewitness was a grocer who claimed to have seen a strange animal prior to 1958, while fishing at Swinney Switch on the Nueces River. According to the grocer, something under the water had taken his hook and gone downstream with it. The man thought he was about to land a trophy after battling the monster with rod and reel for several minutes. Finally, the creature emerged from the water and to the man's shock and horror, climbed onto a sandbar and removed the hook from its mouth. The grocer later described the beast as having, *"both fur and feathers,"* a curious trait. Instinctively, the witness had reached for the pistol that he carried in his tackle box, but the thing flew away just as he was taking aim.

Jerome Clark had also uncovered stories of a monstrous bird that had been haunting the neighbourhood known as the La Palma Colonia in San Benito, since the mid 1940s. When Clark went to the San Benito police station in order to question Officers Galvan and Padilla about their sighting, Lt. Ernest Flores instead showed him a jar that contained alleged Big Bird droppings. According to Lt. Flores, the inch and a half, dry, white lumps had been brought to the police station by an enthusiastic, nineteen year old investigator named Guadalupe Cantu III. Apparently, the droppings had been found by one of Cantu's relatives on the roof of their La Palma home.

I was extremely fortunate to reach Guadalupe by phone during my first trip to the valley in February of 2004. After I had blurted out the name Big Bird, Cantu quietly responded by saying, *"that was a long time ago."* Still, we arranged to meet the next morning. Currently, Guadalupe is a short, stocky, older gentleman, who sometimes wears tinted, yellow glasses, a baseball hat or greying moustache. He has been quite busy over the last thirty years, working as a painter, labourer and raising a family. Cantu immediately struck me as a very likable fellow, pleasant, and polite. He also seemed rather pleased that someone had brought up the subject of `Big Bird` once again after all those years. I know now that my inquiry seemed to renew his interest in the mystery to a large extent. In fact, he was extremely eager to share the news that he had at last seen the Big Bird himself, just seven years earlier.

As we strolled along through the La Palma Colonia with my wife Lori, I listened intently as Guadalupe described how he had been working a night-time paper route, along with his brother-in-

The author with Guadalupe Cantu III in the La Palma Colonia, San Benito

law in the nearby town of Rangerville, when they drove up on a massive, dark, bird perched on a telephone pole. By comparing the bird's height to that of the pole, they were able to estimate that the bird easily stood at least six feet tall. Cantu said that as they watched the huge animal, it flapped its wings once or twice and glided away. He also recalled that, as it departed, the bird appeared to be moving its head from side to side, as if it were scanning the ground for potential prey. Guadalupe described it as being almost black, with a beak like that of an eagle or a hawk, and estimated that it had a fifteen-foot wingspan. He was adamant with me that the bird he saw was not at all common, but seemed close in size to a piper cub aeroplane.

I next began to question Cantu about some of the events that had transpired years before in the La Palma Colonia and he surprised me by remarking, *"I think that there are two different kinds of birds, and I think they're both prehistoric."* I asked him to explain his theory, and he responded by saying that when he had been a young boy in the early 1960s, the monster bird which had frequented his neighbourhood, was usually described as being white or white-breasted, with a scaly look. It looked completely different than the giant, black raptor that *he* had observed.

According to Cantu, the original La Palma bird was often seen perched in a big tree behind his family's home. The creature quickly became a nuisance by emitting a variety of loud, cacophonous, sounds which irritated the neighbourhood dogs to no end, causing them to bark back in retaliation. As a young boy, Guadalupe more or less regarded the winged aberration as some sort of witch or evil spirit, but as he grew older, he began to realize that it was simply a large and unusual animal.

The entire La Palma neighbourhood eventually began to view the bird as evil, until one evening it had even been bold enough to attack an elderly woman by the name of Ignacia, as she went to use her outhouse. Cantu told me that as a boy, he had wanted to go speak with the old woman about her ordeal, but his mother strictly forbade it. Soon after the attack, someone had supposedly tried to shoot the bird with a .22 rifle, but this apparently had no effect on the monster. The unwelcome visitor even had the audacity to distribute its massive droppings on the neighbourhood cars and rooftops on occasion, which is perhaps where Guadalupe's famous stool sample had originated.

Newspaper reports from 1976 confirm that KRIO newsman James Moore did some investigations on his own, and concluded that `Big Bird` was nesting near San Benito at the time. The first documented reports in Cameron County had all emanated from San Benito, including the early morning sighting by Officers Galvan and Padilla. Police reports from the same time period also confirm that a San Benito resident complained of something loud walking on the roof of their house and then stumbling and sliding into their air conditioner. Lieutenant Sam Espárza certainly thought something was going on over San Benito, as did Stan Lawson. Additionally, many of the `Big Bird` reports emanate from nearby areas like Harlingen and Los Fresnos.

When Guadalupe suddenly mentioned the U.F.O. sightings over San Benito, it made me a little uneasy; though inevitably, those of us who attempt to focus on zoological mysteries are frequently thrust into the uncomfortable position of judging eyewitness credibility. However, we must always keep in mind that the people of La Palma are traditional migrant workers, who are very religious, of indigenous stock, and perhaps a bit more connected to the other side. Then again, I considered the possibility that San Benito might be some portal to another dimension, and perhaps I was in over my head. In a phone conversation I had with George Cox, he had mentioned to me that author John Keel had called him back in 1976 to express that there were similarities in the cases of `Big Bird` and West Virginia's Mothman.

After returning home to Houston, Guadalupe began a long campaign of e-mailing me with various updates on `Big Bird`. Initially, he wrote to inform me that many people he knew, including his brother, mother, and several neighbours had heard loud, scary, flying noises that seemed to originate from the treetops in the area. That April, Cantu followed up with an exciting recent development. After a thunderstorm on the evening of the fifth, his cousin Isaias Quintanilla had claimed to have seen `Big Bird` at four in the morning. According to the e-mail, his cousin had stepped outside for a cigarette, when he noticed a bird of mythic proportions perched on a rooftop across the street. According to Isaias, the bird appeared black with a white belly, large, glowing, red eyes, and a three-foot beak. As the creature flapped its wings in a menacing fashion at the witness, he noticed that its outstretched wingspan was wider than the house that it was perched upon. While reading this message for the first time, I was half tempted to drive down immediately, in order to interview Isaias and hopefully even have my very own sighting. Unfortunately, at the time my finances were tight, so I decided to plan for another expedition in the near future.

At the end of May, Guadalupe emailed me to report that `Big Bird` had apparently reappeared once again. This time, a friend of Isaias' named Ricardo, had allegedly been drinking beer with another man in the alley behind Isaias' house. Suddenly and without warning, both men heard a loud swoosh coming from above, and the leaves on the surrounding trees began to shake. The two men were horrified to see a giant bird swoop over their heads, and after realizing that it was the size of a small aeroplane, they quickly bolted into Isaias' house, still shaking from their close encounter.

There was another incident that Guadalupe wrote me about a couple of months later. On July 21st, a friend of Ricardo's claimed that he had seen a bird as tall as a small tree, standing near the banks of the Resaca De La Palma River, which winds through San Benito. This eyewitness supposedly stated that the black, ten-foot tall bird possessed a beak like a parrot, and very large feet. With each e-mail, I began to wonder if perhaps Guadalupe was now having a bit of fun with the over zealous monster hunter, or worse fabricating these stories for his own reasons. But Jerome Clark had painted him as being quite sincere, and besides, Guadalupe assured me that all of these witnesses were real, and that they would be willing to meet with me in person the next time I came to La Palma.

By that fall, Guadalupe's e-mails were starting to take a bizarre twist, and he was beginning to postulate that perhaps `Big Bird` was preying on the neighbourhood cats, and was perhaps even responsible for some missing people in the area. *"Why else would it come so close to town instead of hiding in the nearby woods?"* he wrote me. In one e-mail, he suggested that perhaps I needed to bring a large rifle along when I returned, rather than a camera. In another communication, Guadalupe had mentioned that he had possibly seen U.F.O.s in the area, and it made me wonder again if there were credibility issues. However, he had also explained to me that the U.F. O.s he had seen at night merely looked like stars that seemed to be moving.

In the back of my mind, I was wondering if I was really dealing with a flesh and blood creature, or rather some paranormal phenomenon far beyond my realm of understanding. Guadalupe reassured me by stating more than once that he believed `Big Bird` to be an unusual and intimidating animal, nothing more. I found it uncanny that so many, new reports of `Big Bird` seemed to be coinciding with my resurgent investigation. *"Was it really possible that Big Bird had never actually left?"* I wondered. Despite my burning desire to return to the valley, I was still besieged by commitments and financial restraints.

Guadalupe's continuing neighbourhood investigations eventually turned-up another eyewitness named Markario, who claimed that he was strolling down La Palma Boulevard by the high-school years earlier, when he was accosted by two big, black birds. Markario apparently described the birds as having wings shaped like a bat, adding his attackers also had straight, orange beaks and orange feet. Most puzzling was the eyewitness's claim that the two birds sported some sort of crown or Mohawk similar to a cardinal. Upon further questioning by Guadalupe, Markario recalled that the crowns appeared to be made of skin and bent backwards, like the head crests on pterodactyls.

In one of the most interesting e-mails that I received that following winter, Guadalupe discussed a fleeting `Big Bird` sighting by a La Palma resident who went by the colourful nickname of `Shark`. During his interview, `Shark` had apparently also confessed to having seen a small humanoid creature jump out of a dumpster as he was collecting cans early one morning. He noticed that the *"little vato"* ran rather like a chicken, as it disappeared into a nearby wooded area. Following this strange report, there was a lull in communications from Guadalupe's end. I had wondered if his computer had finally given out, since he had warned me on many occasions that his ability to e-mail me was becoming impaired due to technical issues. At the time, I had other fish to fry, such as dealing with some family illnesses and other obligations.

Subsequently, by the time I was able to finally return to the valley, over two years had passed. A lot of changes had transpired in my life, including the apparent break up of my band and record label. In the interim, Lori and I had decided to undertake two difficult expeditions to the tiny Central American nation of Belize. in order to investigate bigfoot like creatures that had been rumoured to be living in its mountainous jungles. I had also been actively involved in filming a television show, a Canadian documentary about bigfoot. Between all of these extracurricular-activities, and obligations to my employers, it was challenging to find the time to break away, and drive south once again; but eventually, at the beginning of 2006 we did.

As is often the case, Lori, my lovely wife and constant companion, decided to accompany me on the investigation. Our first stop on the drive down was at Swinney Switch, where the alleged incident involving the Corpus Christi grocer and the winged amphibian had taken place. The spot was fairly easy to find, though no doubt it has undergone some changes in the half century that has transpired since the sighting occurred. A statewide drought in Texas was evident at the time of our visit, so the water level seemed low to the point where the river had basically become a marsh at this particular juncture. Some nearby cattle had even taken to grazing in tall, grassy areas that were once underwater.

The author at Swinney Switch on the Nueces River

Having found nothing of interest at Swinney Switch, we next travelled to nearby Robstown, where the first vague reports of 1975 had originated. We almost missed the tiny industrial town, due to it being so unassuming. Our first stop was at the Robstown public library, where I asked the librarian for some archival materials from that period. Unfortunately, the librarian was only able to produce a book on border folklore, but it proved to be slightly helpful. As I explained my purpose, a young Latino man who had overheard my query, politely interjected and informed me that what I sought was actually a local legend known as the `goat-eater`, which was considered to be an owl spirit known as *Lechuza. "If you whistle at a tree that the Lechuza is perched on, it will chase you away,"* the young man explained to me. I later learned that another local interpretation of the Lechuza legend tells of a beautiful maiden drowned herself after being spurned by her lover, and she was reborn as a birdlike creature, soaring through the night, and emitting a long, wailing cry.

The helpful librarian next directed us to the local newspaper office, where a helpful worker dug out the paper archive that dated from when the Robstown bird was supposed to have been reported. Regrettably, I could find no mention of the sightings in any of the issues from that time period. As a result, the newspaper man suggested that we speak with local historian Joe Avalos, a barber who had lived in the town as long as anyone could remember. Mr. Avalos was indeed very gracious, taking us around Robstown and explaining some of the town's history. But, as far as the `Big Bird` legend was concerned, Joe was of the opinion that the entire affair had been merely a fabrication. *"There was no bird,"* he explained to us. *"The legend was based on a Robstown wino who always wore black. The wino became known locally as the Pajaro de Robstown. The man drank so much that he was flying in his head."* Joe told us. *"He burned up in a house on Pechadder Avenue."* Mr. Avalos also informed us that he had a CD with a song about the *Pajaro de Grande*, if we would like a copy.

Because we had a long journey ahead, we declined, and continued on to our motel in San Benito, which would serve as our home base for the coming days. A billboard as we drove into town proudly proclaimed that San Benito was the hometown of country music star Freddie Fender. Upon our arrival, I was happy to realize that our motel was actually in a great location, just a mile or two north of the La Palma Colonia, where the `Big Bird` was perhaps still being sighted. Merely a mile or two to the north of our motel lay Harlingen's Ed Carey Road, where Jackie Davies and Tracey Lawson had their sighting. Because the surrounding landscape seemed flat, and the sky quite large, I decided to deploy a small, infared surveillance camera outside of our second story window, just for kicks. I aimed the camera at a large field adjacent to our building, and rigged up a monitor in my room, so that we would see anything large that flew by.

Just as I was setting the camera, Lori shouted out that she had just seen a large, white owl fly by outside of our room. Based on her level of excitement, I could tell that she was quite sincere in what she had observed. Coincidentally, it had only been a few hours earlier when we had heard about owls from the young man in Robstown, which made Lori's sighting seem somewhat significant. I also remembered that Guadalupe had mentioned a Big Bird witness who had uttered the word *Tecolote*, which can translate to owl in Spanish.

My adrenalin was pumping that night, so I decided to sit for a while outside in the darkness, perched on the edge of a ditch adjacent to a large field. As usual, I was armed with my night vision and video camera. I found myself surrounded by the hypnotic drone of the chirping insects,

Barber Joe Avalos sits in front of the Robstown cantina

and began to wonder if there really could actually be some kind of prehistoric animal flying over the area on occasion. Needless to say, it was a restless night once my head hit the pillow back in my room. My thoughts ran on and on endlessly, as I contemplated what lay ahead or what I might learn from the continuing investigation.

The next morning, I awoke at the crack of dawn and dressed quietly as not to awake Lori. I decided to take a drive out to the spot where James Thompson had reported seeing a "rhamphorynchoid" back in 1983. Because of the similarities to the Guzman case, I somehow felt a special connection to this particular incident. I had retraced Thompson's route on the previous trip, but some new information had given me a more approximate location of the actual encounter. The remote spot on Highway 100 was just as I had imagined. The surrounding landscape was flat, and the adjacent field was now teeming with corn stalks. Some interspersed palm trees gave the locale somewhat of a marshy, Cretaceous feel. The humidity there was such that I had trouble taking a photo, because my lens would fog up the instant after being wiped dry. Traffic was sparse that morning, enabling me to envision some strange animal winging through the area without too much disruption.

Lawson had been among the first to encounter `Big Bird`. I was pleasantly surprised to come upon a bird sanctuary that is located there, adjacent to the Colorado Arroyo River. The Harlingen Arroyo Colorado Birding Centre is part of a network that has been set-aside for avid bird watchers in south Texas, due to the hundreds of bird species that inhabit the area during various parts of the year. The dense, shrubby trees definitely seemed abuzz with numerous species of chirping birds. As I made my way down to the river, I was struck by how dense the surrounding brush was. The overgrown riverbank definitely reminded me of some of the jungle creeks in Central America that I had hiked. While resting by the river, I managed to observe plenty of lizards and bird, but nothing sizeable.

On the return trip to my car, I stopped and spoke with one of the caretakers, who was busy planting flowers along the trail. He informed me that his name was Mark Conway and that he was an employee of the birding centre, as well as being an avid birder himself. I explained that I was researching for a book on the Big Bird and he suggested that I might consider the Jabiru stork (*Jabiru mycteria*) as a candidate for some of the reports. Mark explained that Jabirus, which fly north to the Valley from Central America during the late summer and early fall, can easily stand five feet tall, and display a wingspan in excess of eight feet. I myself was fortunate to observe a Jabiru stork, on my most recent trip back to the Valley, and they do seem quite large. However, it would be unprecedented for these storks to be around in January, when the bulk of `Big Bird` sightings in the Valley had occurred.

After breakfast, Lori and I visited the Harlingen Library, and as I had hoped, I found several old newspaper articles pertaining to `Big Bird`. In the article about the James Thompson sighting, the reporter mentions Thompson's employer as being Emergency Medical Services, and lists an address in Harlingen. For kicks, Lori and I decided to drive by, and were surprised to see that E.M. S. was in fact still there. The administrator on sight there did not have any information on James Thompson's present whereabouts, and assured me that no current employees would have been

The author standing in front of an ambulance similar to James Thompson's

employed around that time. While in Harlingen, I also contacted KGBT, the television station that reportedly had broadcast some film of `Big Bird's` nine-inch tracks back in 1976. An employee informed me that, unfortunately, there were no archives kept from that period, since the medium of that time was film, and no one had thought to preserve anything until the digital age. Therefore, since VCRs were non-existent in 1976, we have probably lost a precious piece of photographic evidence forever.

Next, Lori and I drove towards the border, as I had an appointment with Kevin Garcia - a reporter from the *Brownsville Herald.* I had contacted Kevin after reading a Halloween article he had written. It had been about the valley's legendary goblins, which are known as the *Cucuy.* In his article, Kevin had cited a `Big Bird` witness named Alex Resendez, of whom I had not been previously aware. I was anxious to see what other new information he might have for me. Kevin is an exceedingly bright and articulate young man, who explained that he has a special interest in folklore. After a brief but productive conversation, Garcia mentioned that he was in a bit of a hurry and asked if he could perhaps call me later for an interview, to which I readily agreed. He also gave me the contact information for a local author and paranormal researcher named Lynn David Livsey, who headed an organization known as the `Enlightenment Society`, which apparently holds regular meetings where `Big Bird` is often the topic of conversation.

After leaving Brownsville, we finally decided that it was time to pay Guadalupe a visit. He had not been answering his phone, nor had he responded to any of my e-mails. As a result, I was concerned about his well-being and unsure what to expect. Upon arrival, his wife answered the door after a few moments, and Guadalupe appeared a little while later. Any concerns that I had were soon dispensed of as we caught up on events.

He informed me that the eyewitness named Ricardo had unfortunately gone to prison, but we strolled across the street to Isaias' house in order to see if he was around. The woman who answered his door informed us in Spanish that Isias was sleeping. As we began to leave, Guadalupe explained that Isaias had no doubt been drinking, and that he and Ricardo were examples of the rampant drug-abuse and alcoholism that plague the impoverished residents of La Palma.

Our best chance seemed to be Markario. After a short drive to his last known residence, we did find his uncle, who directed us to yet another address, where we met up with Markario's brother, who goes by the name of `Shy`. `Shy`, so-called due to his quiet manner, seemed uncomfortable with the subject of `Big Bird`, and Guadalupe whispered to me that `Shy's` wife Natalie had been attacked once, and that they subsequently did not like to discuss it. Natalie could be seen pacing inside the house, listening intently, but unwilling to come out and speak with us. `Shy` did tell us in Spanish, that about a year and a half earlier, he had heard a loud, flapping, noise that shook his house, as if something large was flying over. This had happened at around 11:00 p.m.

After leaving `Shy's` residence, we drove to an apartment where we were told we might find Makario, but the occupant there informed us that Markario was out running around somewhere, and that he could possibly be with Isaias. Since it was now apparent that we were merely going in circles, my hope began to evaporate quickly. Irregardless of this fiasco, I still get the feeling that Guadalupe has been sincere in everything that he has told me. Nor do I doubt in his desire to prove that `Big Bird` really exists.

The house on which Isaias Quintanilla claims to have seen Big Bird

Before leaving La Palma, we made one last stop at the home of Guadalupe's elderly mother, who, we were told, was feeling a little under the weather. The tiny Mexican woman got out of bed to greet us, which made me feel a little guilty. She explained to us in Spanish that she had often heard loud, flapping sounds through the years, and that she believed it to be the `Big Bird`. Sometimes, she went on, there were even loud thuds on her roof, as if something large had landed. Guadalupe confirmed that he had seen what looked to be oversized bird droppings on her property. Unlike the droppings from 1976, these were apparently yellow and runny. As we departed La Palma, the idea of mounting a couple of motion-activated cameras during my next visit, was discussed.

On our return trip to Houston, Lori and I stopped in San Antonio, where I was able to pin point the probable location of the sighting by the three schoolteachers, during February of 1976. I knew from one newspaper article, that the incident had taken place in the Southside School District. I deduced the probable route that the three teachers would have driven to the school complex, if they had been driving from the populated, metropolitan, area to the north. As described in the articles, the route was somewhat isolated. In one particular spot about two miles north of the school, there were indeed some cows grazing under power lines, exactly as described. Not surprisingly, there was also the San Antonio River flowing nearby. Even though some thirty years has passed, the surrounding area still appears rural and forested. I was able to arrange a meeting with a school official named Nancy Thompson, who seemed fascinated by the whole affair. As expected though, the present whereabouts of the three teachers remains unknown. Their names were not familiar to anyone on the present staff, and none of the current employees had been working there back in 1976.

Within a couple of weeks, I had returned to the valley once again, in order to speak before a meeting of the `Enlightenment Society`. As promised, Kevin Garcia had written an article for the *Brownsville Herald* a few days earlier that had covered my revised interest in the `Big Bird` legend, as well as announcing my upcoming visit. The result was that a good crowd had gathered to hear me speak at the Shoney's Restaurant in Brownsville where the free event was being held.

I began my lecture by discussing bigfoot, as well as my Belizean hominid research, since both host and author Livsey, as well as the audience, seemed to be interested in the subject. I then presented a slide show that basically went over everything I had found out about `Big Bird`. The highlight of the event was when `Big Bird` eyewitness Alex Resendez got up and recounted the two `Big Bird` sightings that he claimed to have had in the 1970s. At the conclusion, several people from the audience approached me. One was an elderly Hispanic man, who claimed to be a friend of eyewitness Alverico Guajardo. He assured me that Alverico had indeed encountered something dreadful that January night back in 1976. Next, another audience member introduced himself, and confided in me that his brother had seen a weird animal flying near Los Fresnos, near where James Thompson had his sighting. The man confided that like Thompson, his brother had described the animal he saw as resembling a pterosaur.

Chapter 4

- Flying Things Worldwide -

We would be truly remiss in our survey of Texas' airborne monsters, if we failed to mention one that has definitely been proven to be real. True, it was over sixty million years ago, but a massive pterosaur by the name of *Quetzalcoatlus northropi* may have been one of the largest animals ever to fly over Earth. [5] This aeroplane-sized creature sported a whopping forty-foot wingspan, and may have weighed close to two hundred pounds. Its fossilized remains were unearthed in Big Bend National Park by palaeontologist Dr. Douglas Lawson during 1975. The curious timing of this event may indeed have had an impact on the collective psyche of some `Big Bird` eyewitnesses, a theory that will be addressed at the conclusion.

It goes without saying that the existence of winged, prehistoric reptiles in modern Texas seems to be a far-fetched proposition. The idea is quite understandably a difficult concept for most to accept, as it goes against everything that we were taught in school. Keep in mind however, that humans are far from omnipotent. Our understanding of this planet is an ongoing process that will never be wholly complete. Science and history books are constantly being revised as new discoveries are made. It is arrogance, particularly from the conservative scientific establishment, which prevents us from considering ideas that go against their established theories. The number of new animal species that continue to be discovered could easily fill volumes of encyclopaedias, though most are unaware of this fact. Therefore, the possibility that small populations of pterosaurs have eluded modern discovery is worth at least an iota of consideration, especially when we examine the reports on a global scale.

Africa is well-known for its many enduring natural mysteries. Relatively little is known about some remote parts of the `Dark Continent`, particularly its unexplored jungles and swamps, which remain some of the most impenetrable places on earth. Cryptozoologists who search for new animal species are familiar with many African legends having to do with fabulous beasts. One such legend extends into modern times and involves a winged monster known as the *kongamato.* Traveller Frank H. Melland first brought the *kongamato* notoriety in 1923, when he mentioned it in his book titled *In Witchbound Africa.* According to Melland, both the Kaonde and Bokaonde tribes of northwestern Rhodesia (now Zambia), believed that there was a sinister flying lizard that haunted the Jiundu swamps. The creature's name translated from the Kaonde tongue meant "Overwhelmer of Boats," due to the monster's habit of attacking humans travelling in canoes. It was believed that to encounter *kongamato* meant almost certain death.

Superficially, the animal was said to somewhat resemble a bird. But, the *kongamato's* reddish body and membranous, bat-like wings were described as being smooth and bare. In addition, its beak was said to be lined with sharp little teeth. The *kongamato's* wingspan was said to be anywhere from four to seven feet across. In his classic book, *On the Track of Unknown Animals,* The late Dr. Bernard Heuvelmans pointed out that the Kaonde's use of the word lizard might indicate that Kongamato possessed a reptilian tail. When Melland played upon a hunch and showed the Kaonde natives some illustrations of pterosaurs, they quickly responded, *"Kongamato!"*

The Kongomato of Africa has been described as looking like a pterosaur

From the south of the former Rhodesia, there is a published account from 1925, which tells of a possible *kongamato* attack on a solitary, brave warrior who had penetrated a dark swamp. According to the account, the man had emerged from the swamp with a deep, chest wound and claimed that a monster has pierced his flesh with its beak Later, when the bed ridden victim was shown a book containing a drawing of a pterosaur, he supposedly leapt out of his bed in terror, fleeing the house that he was recovering in.

In a 1928 composition titled *A Game Ranger on Safari,* author A. Blayney Percival writes of the Kitui Wakamaba, a tribe living near Mount Kenya that greatly feared a huge, winged monster with a heavy tail. The Kitui Wakamba had frequently found the animal's unusual tracks wherever it had landed, and they had also seen its large silhouette against the night sky. During 1942, Colonel Charles R.S. Pitman backed up the Kongamato stories that were coming out of northern Rhodesia in his book *A Game Warden Takes Stock.* Renowned ichthyologist Dr. J.L.B. Smith, writing about the rediscovered Coelacanth (which like the pterosaurs, were believed to have gone extinct millions of years ago), recounted tales of flying dragons near Tanzania's Mount Kilimanjaro. Don't forget the detailed 1956 sighting by engineer J.P.F. Brown, that was mentioned in chapter one. Shortly after Brown's report was published, Mr. and Mrs. D. McGregor wrote to a local newspaper, claiming that they had also seen large "flying lizards" in southern Rhodesia, between Bulawayo and Livingstone.

Travelling up Africa's Gold Coast exists another intriguing animal known as the *susabonsam*. According to the locals, the *susabonsam* resembles a man with the wings of a bat. In his book *Investigating the Unexplained*, zoologist Ivan Sanderson wrote about being dive-bombed by an apparently enormous, black bat with a twelve-foot wingspan while wading in an African creek. The incident took place in Cameroon's Assumbo Mountains during 1932. [6] Sanderson soon learned the natives referred to the creature as the *oliatu* and that they were greatly panicked by its appearance. There were three other witnesses to Sanderson's attack, including biologist Gerald Russell, who shot at the animal but failed to bring it down. This incident led to speculation by Sanderson, Heuvelmans and others that the *oliatu*, *susabonsam* and k*ongamato* would all eventually be proven to be unknown species of giant bats. Sanderson was quite adamant that what attacked him was not a pterosaur and he did not want other researchers jumping to that conclusion. My thoughts on the giant bat theory will be addressed in chapter six. [7]

The only dedicated African pterosaur expedition to date took place in the summer of 1988, when renowned cryptozoologist Dr. Roy Mackal of the University of Chicago. travelled to the south-western African nation of Namibia. [8] Mackal had led an earlier, well-publicised expedition that had searched for living dinosaurs in the Congo seven years earlier. This time, he had been lured back to Africa by a group of German settlers who had described a leathery, flying creature with a thirty-foot wingspan living in their remote desert region. Although Mackal never managed to spot the animal himself during his visit, his associate James Kosi claimed that he witnessed, *"A large, black glider with white markings, distantly flying between some hilltops."* Coincidentally, Namibia's *Namaqua* tribe believes in a legend about a giant, flying snake. The animal is said to be comparable to a large, speckled python, but with bat-like wings just below its head, which also has two horns. Supposedly, there is even a flying snake attack, which involved a young sheep herder named Michael Esteruise. During January of 1942, Esteruise was apparently found unconscious, claiming that a huge snake had sprung out of a cave, landing on top of him, before flying away.

Living-dinosaur enthusiast Dr. Kent Hovind tells of how, at a lecture he was giving one time, he was approached by a young man identifying himself as an exchange student from Kenya. To Dr. Hovind's amazement, the student informed him that pterosaurs were fairly common near his village back in Africa. So much so in fact, that the student was not aware they were thought to be extinct.

From another lost world, the volcanic, jungle islands of Papua New Guinea, come other reports of living pterosaurs. The *ropen*, as it is known first, came to light following an initial expedition by Scottish adventurer Bill Gibbons, who like Mackal had previously pursued dinosaurs in Africa. Soon, other investigators such as Carl Baugh, Paul Nation, Jonathan Whitcomb and others would mount expeditions of their own. Interestingly, all of these spiritual men are young earth proponents or creationists, who feel that the *ropen's* existence if proven, will help substantiate the Bible's claim that the Earth and all its animals are the result of divine design which occurred a mere six thousand years ago. This of course, contradicts the theory of evolution, which states that a mass extinction event took place millions of years ago and that certain species were able to survive by adapting to the changing conditions. The creationists also like to point to Biblical references about fiery, winged serpents and dragons as further proof that pterosaurs are still among us.

From the islands of Umboi and Rambutyo, which lie just east of Papua New Guinea, come more reports of the *ropen* or "Demon Flyer," whose description is startlingly similar to that of the *kongamato*, as well as the rhamphorhynchoids. For example, the *ropen's* wingspan is often said to be only four feet across. In addition, it is described as having a mouth filled with sharp, little teeth. Most notably, mention is made of a long, serpent-like tail, with a distinct shape on the end. The natives greatly fear the *ropen*, which is often said to attack funeral processions, due to an attraction to the scent of decaying flesh. In a similar fashion, the creatures will reportedly dive bomb the local fisherman's nets, in an attempt to pillage their catch. The *ropen* is said to be nocturnal and to live in high mountain caves. The locals on Rambutyo explain how encounters were commonplace about thirty years ago, particularly on the unexplored, eastern side of the island. On Umboi Island, which lies to the south of Rambutyo, there have been recent sightings, particularly around Mount Bel and on the western coast. The entire village of Gomlongon reportedly watched a *ropen* fly over a jungle valley and out to sea during 1995.

One of the most diligent *ropen* investigators has been a court videographer from California named Jonathan Whitcomb, who has written a book titled *The Ropen: In Search of Living Pterosaurs*. Whitcomb has managed to interview numerous witnesses on Umboi, including a group of men who encountered a large *ropen* when they were boys. Gideon Koro, as well as his brother Wesley, and their friend Mesa, were hiking near volcanic Lake Pung around 1994, when they claim that they spotted a *ropen* with a twenty foot wingspan and a series of bumps or ridges running down the entire length of its back The animal also had a long tail, according to Gideon. A western missionary named Jim Blume has collected numerous reports in the region, including an incident where a local man was allegedly attacked and killed by a *ropen* while working in his garden during the 1980s. From nearby Goodenough Island, there is a documented *ropen* sighting by the school's headmaster.

On the mainland of New Guinea, there is mention of a gigantic version of the *ropen* known as the *duah*, which reportedly boasts a twenty-foot wingspan, as well as leathery skin. According to some witnesses, the *duah* also possesses a bony head crest reminiscent of the fossil form pteranodon. Much like the smaller *ropen*, it has apparently acquired a taste for decomposing flesh. It is said to sweep in under cover of night and empty the graves of the recently buried. The *duah* has even been accused of carrying-off an occasional villager. A most remarkable detail that has been mentioned in regards to both the *ropen* and the *duah,* is their apparent ability to emit a bright glow that can be seen at night from some distance. This seemingly, fabulous attribute has been written off as being either the result of highly reflective scales that react to the moonlight, or perhaps a type of bioluminescent fungus growing on the animal's skin. In either case, many fishermen have claimed they've seen the eerie, glowing apparitions flying over the water at night. As strange as this attribute sounds, a glowing light has been linked with Namibia's flying snake, as well as the fiery serpents mentioned in the bible.

There is a fascinating report by an American G.I. named Duane Hodgkinson, who was stationed near Finschafen, New Guinea in 1944. Hodgkinson recounts, how along with a companion, he chanced upon a prehistoric animal while out exploring. Hodginson wrote, *"On this one particular trip we had the opportunity to witness a pterodactyl take off from the ground, and then circle back overhead, giving us a perfect view, which clearly showed the long beak and appendage protruding from the back of its head. It was a big one! I have a Piper aeroplane, which has a wingspread of twenty-six feet, and it appeared to be about that size. The frequency of its wing flaps*

Expeditions in search of New Guinea's mysterious Ropen are ongoing

was estimated to be about one or two seconds. With each flap we could hear a loud swish, swish and the plants and brush immediately beneath its take off path were deflected by the down rush of air." Hodgkinson later added that he didn't recall whether the creature had a tail, but that it *did* possess a long neck.

Since meeting at a conference at which we were both lecturing, I have been in regular correspondence with *ropen* researcher named Paul Nation. Nation is smart and tough, a former ostrich handler who is, as of this writing, in the process of mounting yet another expedition to New Guinea to search for evidence. Paul is of the opinion that the *ropen* is related to the fossil Dimorphodon, which is a fossil rhamphorhynchoid which possessed unusual dentition, and a six foot wingspan. Because of its elongated leg bones, Dimorphodon may have been extremely adept at moving around on the ground.

To the south of New Guinea, there is a detailed report from Perth in Western Australia. A married couple claimed that they spotted a living pterosaur soaring above the coastline one evening during December of 1997. In her statement, the wife Penny wrote, *"Within a minute or so it had reached our position and was about 250 or 300 feet above us and slightly inland. The area was moderately well lit and I saw that it seemed to be a light reddish-tan colour. It did not appear to be covered with feathers but had a leathery texture. Soon after it passed us it flew over a more brightly lit sports area which highlighted even more the leathery appearance also bringing more detail to view. The wings were the most definite leathery feature, they were shaped in a triangular arch, similar to a very elongated shark fin, The body also still appeared leathery, though textured as though possibly covered with fine hair or small scales, the distance preventing any finer observation than that it was slightly different texture than the wings. The shape of the body was a streamlined torpedo shape, slightly broadest at the chest and tapering slightly back to the hip, then tapering more quickly after the hips to a moderately thing tail which was slightly longer than the body."* The wife estimated that the creature's wingspan was in excess of thirty feet, though she admitted it is difficult to make an accurate calculation at that distance.

Travelling up the Indo Pacific towards mainland Asia, there is a flying monster that is reported from the island of Cerram. It is known as the *orang bati*, which translates to "man-bat" in the local Molluccan patois. As the name implies, the creature is described as being slightly humanoid, as well as possessing leathery wings. The *orang bati* is said to dwell in caves high up on Mount Kairatu. The nearby island of Java boasts a similar beast known as the giant *ahool*, which the natives compare to a giant bat, due to the *ahool's* membranous wings with attached claws. Its head is described as being similar to a monkey. The dark, grey *ahool* apparently draws its name from its unique call, which sounds just like its name. Orinthologist M.E.G. Bartels claimed he actually heard a specimen vocalizing in 1925, while hiking in the Salek Mountains on the western side of the island. As with the *kongamato*, some of the comparisons to bats cannot be ignored; but the problem *is* that the locals are familiar with the flying fox, the largest bat species known to man. Thus, these winged monsters appear to be something quite different.

Asia, and particularly the Far East, possess a great wealth of dragonlore. One contemporary dragon account involves an English teacher named David Nardiello, who was bicycling home in Watagh Shinke-Cho, Japan, during May of 2003. It was raining heavily when Nardiello said he noticed a creature rising out of a flooded rice paddy. He later described the animal as being white, with the body and tail of a lizard and the legs of a cat. Nardiello claimed that the creature possessed the head of a snake set atop a long neck. He also noticed that it had sharp fangs and black eyes, as well as leathery, bat wings. Nadiello watched in horror as the thing shot up into the sky. Later that night, he looked out his apartment window and thought that he saw the thing flying by again.

On the continent of Europe there are also modern pterosaur reports on record. While this may seem harder to swallow than - say - the unexplored jungles of Africa or the Indo Pacific, keep in mind that many pterosaur fossils have been found throughout the European continent. In addition, Europe possesses a rich history of dragon legends. John Goertzen, yet another creationist out to disprove evolution, has written an interesting essay which proposes that a rhamphorhynchoid known as *Scaphognathus crassirosstris* survived in Europe until the 17th Century. In his essay, Goertzen quotes the Greek historian Herodotus, (484 BC–ca.425 BC) who once wrote, *"There is a place in Arabia, situated very near the city of Buto, to which I went, on hearing of some winged serpents; and when I arrived there, I saw bones and spines of serpents, in such quantities as it would be impossible to describe. The form of the serpent is like that of the water-snake; but he has wings without feathers, and as like as possible to the wings of a bat."*

Goertzen also references several ancient artifacts, including four Egyptian seals, as well as Roman coins, Old World maps, and a French wood carving that seem to clearly depict pterosaurs. In addition, he quotes naturalists such as Prosper Alpin, [9] who described winged dragons in Egypt during the 16th Century. Based on recurring references to long, vaned, tails, as well as head crests, Goertzen concludes that the pterosaur known as Scaphognathus is a likely candidate. At the time he wrote his essay, Scaphognathus was the only known rhamphorhynchoid with a head crest. However, within the past two years, paleontologists have discovered another species known as Pterorynchus, which shares both of these important characteristics.

There is a widely disseminated story that appeared in the *Illustrated London News* on February 9th, 1856. Though the account is widely thought to be yet another example of sensational story telling, I include it here for the sake of posterity. The article states that, *"A discovery of great scientific importance has just been made at Culmout (France). Some men employed in cutting a tunnel to unite the St. Dizier and Nancy Railways, had just thrown down an enormous block of stone by means of gunpowder, and were in the act of breaking it to pieces, when from a cavity in it they suddenly saw emerge a living being of monstrous form. This creature, which belongs to the class of animals hitherto considered to be extinct, has a very long neck, and a mouth filled with sharp teeth. It stands on four legs, which are united together by two membranes, doubtless intended to support the animal in the air, and are armed with four claws terminated by long and crooked talons. Its general form resembles that of a bat, differing only in its size, which is that of a large goose. Its membranous wings, when spread out, measure from tip to tip three metres twenty-two centimetres. Its colour is a livid black; its skin is naked; thick and oily; its intestines only contain a colourless liquid like clear water. On reaching the light the monster gave some signs of life, by shaking its wings, but soon expired, uttering a hoarse cry. This strange creature, to which may be given the name of a living fossil, has been brought to Grey, where a naturalist well versed in the study of palaeontology, immediately recognized it as belonging to the genus Pterodactylanas..."* Since there is no other record of what happened to this potentially important specimen, we should assume the whole story is merely a fabrication.

From the Greek Island of Crete, where one might seem as likely to encounter a mythical harpy as a living pterosaur, three young bird-hunters claimed that they encountered the latter. The three boys were hiking near a river in the Asterousia Mountains on the western side of the island at around 8:30 in the morning, during the summer of 1986. Imagine their surprise, when Manolis Calaitzis, Nikolaos Chalkiadakis and Nikolasos Sfakianakis observed a giant, dark grey bird, with bat-like wings (that included finger-like projections) fly overhead. The unidentified animal also displayed claw-like talons, and a beak similar to a pelican, according to the witnesses. Overall, it reminded the boys all of a pterodactyl. Perhaps if the young hunters had been able to get of a shot off, we would have physical proof that pterosaurs are indeed still living.

Great Britain, for a well-populated island, certainly has its fair share of strange indigenous beasties, including the winged weirdo known as the Owlman. So, it should come as little surprise that there are also a fair number of apparent pterosaur reports emanating from the United Kingdom. In *Dragons: More Than a Myth?* cryptozoologist Richard Freeman recounts, *"In September, 1982 a freakish animal was appearing in the skies above the Aire Valley in West Yorkshire. It was first spotted in a wooded area known as the devil's punchbowl on the 12th of September. It flew low on erratically large, bat like wings and according to the witness, resembled a pterodactyl."* Sightings of the Yorkshire pterodactyl apparently continued until 1985, with eyewitnesses generally describing it as appearing grey or black, with a five to eight foot wingspan.

In the west London suburb of Brentford, there were reports of a creature known as the Brentford Griffin. The whole affair began in 1984, when a man by the name of Kevin Chippendale was walking down Braemar Road around five o'clock one evening. According to Chippendale, he spotted an animal which resembled a large dog with wings. Several months later, Chippendale sighted the winged apparition again, as well as another eyewitness, prompting the local press to run a story about the colourful monster. In a later interview, Chippendale recalled that the griffin's skin was smooth and that its wings appeared to be bat-like.

In his book, Freeman also mentions other pterosaur sightings from Great Britain, including reports from Southport Parks employees during 1999. As recently as 2004, paranormal author Nick Redfern had received a letter from British resident Steve Nicklin who wrote, *"Me and a friend saw a humanoid greyish figure with a human-type head standing in a tree. We estimated its size at around seven feet. It had two legs and two arms connected to membrane-type wings. Its clawed arms seemed connected to these wings, a bit like a pterosaur. It moved its head and looked directly at us, since the moon was full and there were street lights not far away. It turned its head from us, took one giant leap and glided to the next tree. The tree bent under the creature's weight as it took the impact."*

From South America, there is a curious encounter on record from the vast, unexplored Amazon Basin, where one might expect to hear about such things. The primary eyewitness was a Liverpool man named J. Harrison, though there were apparently others present. During February of 1947, Harrison was apparently boating on the Manuos River, a tributary of the mighty Amazon, when he spotted five, strange looking birds overhead. The animals in question were brown and leathery, with twelve-foot wingspans. Harrison noticed that the creature's wings were apparently ribbed, while the heads were flat and attached to long necks. Subsequently, it has been suggested that perhaps what Harrison observed was a group of storks. The jungles of South America have long been rumoured to harbour lost civilizations and living dinosaurs. Having camped along the Manuos River as a youth back in 1977, I can attest to the Amazon's mysterious qualities.

Evidence of relict pterosaurs in South America can be found on the controversial carvings known as the Ica stones of Peru. A local physician named Dr. Javier Cabrera believes that the thousands of intricately carved stones may be ancient, though their true age can not be scientifically validated. Some of the stones may, in fact, be fakes, generated by local artisans trying to capitalize on the tourists. The original stones were allegedly discovered by a farmer near the mysterious Nazca lines back in the 1960s. Many of the carvings portray humans living along side dinosaurs. A few stones in particular, display obvious renditions of men riding on the backs of living pterodactyls.

Starting in 1995, reports of a vicious, unknown predator known as the *Chupacabras* began surfacing throughout Puerto Rico and Latin America. Reports vary as to what the "goat sucker," which is said to mutilate livestock, really looks like. Early on, the *Chupacabras* was described as looking reptilian or possibly even extraterrestrial. Later, it took on the form of a canine, with bristly hairs or spikes running down its back. Eventually, some eyewitnesses even began to describe bat-like wings. While searching the internet, I discovered an organization calling itself `The Pterodactyl Society`, whose website proclaims that *Chupacabras* creatures that have been reported from Puerto Rico may in fact be members of the species Batrachognathus, a toothy pterosaur known from Jurrasic fossils. Batrachognathus had a flat face that might have resembled a bat or monkey. The *Chupacabras* is sometimes referred to as the "hell monkey" in the Sonoran desert.

There is a familiar ring to the string of recent *Chupacabras* sightings that have come out of Chile in the past three years. On July 23rd of 2003, three boys named Diego, Carlos and Jonathan were having a sleepover at Diego's grandfather's house near San Pedro de Atacama, when they heard an eerie scratching noise coming from outside the door. After getting up their collective nerve and looking outside, the boys claimed they witnessed a menacing apparition standing only fifty feet away. They would later describe the monster as standing about five feet tall, with the wings of a bat, and talons for feet. The boys claimed that the animal was shiny, black, and smooth with an eleven-foot wingspan. It also appeared to have a beak, large black eyes, and a crest on its head. Supposedly, when the creature took off, the surrounding foliage shook from the gusts of wind that were created.

Earlier that month, a Chilean man named Juan Acuqa told police that he was attacked by two hideous monsters while walking home late at night in the town of Parral. *"They were both dog-faced and had wings,"* remarked Acuqa, who jumped into a canal to escape his attacker's strong claws. His injuries apparently caused him to be briefly hospitalized. During August, the Abbett de la Torre Diaz family was driving through Chile's Pampa Acha region, when they observed four animals that resembled "dog-faced kangaroos" moving through the air. The father described the four creatures as looking like birds, with dog-like heads, and backswept wings. He compared them to gargoyles. The entire family became understandably terrified during their disturbing encounter.

Is it possible that some well-hidden pterosaurs may occasionally stray from their home in the jungles of the Amazon or Mesoamerica? During the 1980s, cryptozoologist Loren Coleman investigated reports of high-flying pterodactyls that were coming out of Mexico's Yucatan Peninsula and concluded that witnesses were probably misidentifying frigate birds. However, a close examination of the reports and legends of North America seems to indicate that there may, indeed, be something afoot.

Chapter 5

- More American Legends and Reports -

It now seems we can truly make a case that creatures resembling - presumably extinct - pterosaurs have been observed by humans all over the world for thousands of years. Dramatic encounters with these amazing animals may have resulted in many of the fabulous legends about winged dragons. One such icon that is significant, is the Aztec god Quetzalcoatl, who is often portrayed as a feathered serpent. The deity's likeness can be found on ornate carvings at the ruins of Teotihuacan near Mexico City. To his worshippers, Quetzalcoatl was an omnipotent ruler of the ancient skies, who was greatly feared. Coincidentally, the land of the Aztecs is relatively close to Big Bird's haunt in south Texas. In fact, as we saw in the last chapter, when the fossilized remains of an enormous pterodactyl were unearthed in west Texas during 1975, the giant, new species was anointed *Quetzalcoatlus northropi*. The Aztecs were not the only early Mexican civilization to worship a winged creature either. The ancient ruins of El Tajin near Veracruz display carvings that look astoundingly like a pterosaur.

There are other legends as well. In addition to Quetzacoatl, the Aztecs also had tales that spoke of a flying demon named Izpuzteque, as well as a giant bird that foretold the coming of their Spanish conquerors. The Navaho people of the American southwest believed in pterosaur-like creatures, according to cryptozoologist Nick Sucik. The Tzeltal tribe of Latin America feared the Ikals, which were said to be small, hairy, flying beings that sometimes attacked humans, especially women.

The Illini tribe of the Mississippi Valley believed in a flying dragon of sorts. Known as the Piasa, the monster's massive images had been painted on a cliff face overlooking the Mississippi River near Alton, Illinois sometime prior to the 17th century. Early people, who were obviously aware that the Piasa was a highly unusual animal, had painted the ancient petroglyphs there. The Piasa was portrayed as having bat-wings, a bearded, man-like face and an extremely long tail, which ended in a fin. Author Perry Armstrong was the first to draw comparisons between the Piasa and the rhamphorhynchoids in his book *The Piasa, or the Devil among the Indians,* published in 1887.

Accounts of so-called "flying snakes" can be found in Western newspapers during the late 19th century. Whether these reports stem from actual encounters with archaic, flying reptiles, or are the result of sensational reporting remains to be seen, since some of the accounts note the absence of wings! Irregardless, Nick Sucik was kind enough to forward this article to me. *"One day in June of 1873, a farmer in Bonham, Texas looked up from his work and was astonished at what he saw. There appeared to be an enormous flying snake, banded with brilliant yellow stripes, writhing and twisting in the sky above him. Other people in the Bonham vicinity also observed this strange apparition, which was said to be at least as long as a telegraph pole. According to the report in `The Enterprise`, the bewildered eyewitnesses watched the creature coil itself up, and thrust forward its enormous head as if striking at something."* Loren Coleman wrote about this same incident in *Curious Encounters,* as well as similar sightings that had apparently transpired in Kansas (1873) and South Carolina (1888).

There is yet another newspaper article that may hold an important clue in the lore of American thunderbirds. [10] The article first appeared in the *Tombstone Epitaph* on April 26, 1890. According to the now famous account, a pair of ranchers riding on horseback came across a flying monster in the Whetstone Mountains near Arizona's Huachuca Desert a few days earlier. The monster appeared to be mortally wounded, enabling the ranchers to finish the creature off with their rifles. Upon close examination, the thing was reportedly enormous, with an unbelievable wingspan of a hundred and sixty feet! The monster, which basically resembled a pterodactyl, was described as completely hairless, with membranous wings and a head like an alligator. The shooters noted that it had huge eyes as big as dinner plates and two horse-like legs. Due to the animal's immense size, the ranchers apparently were only able to return to Tombstone with the tip of one wing that they had cut off.

The whole incident could have easily been written off as the result of sensational journalism. However, in 1969, a man named Harry McClure came forward to confirm that the report was basically true, since he had heard about the incident as a boy, growing up in nearby Lordsburg, New Mexico. McClure clarified the situation by explaining that in reality, the animal had only possessed a twenty to thirty foot wingspan, and that the creature had not been killed by the ranchers after all, but had actually escaped. The entire saga has been further muddled by claims that an actual photograph exists, which shows a dead pterodactyl with its wings being stretched out against a barn. A few men in vintage clothing may also appear in the picture. In the past several years, there have been some clearly fake reconstructions of the alleged photo, in circulation, including one that alleges to show some Civil War soldiers, along with a cadaver. However, despite all efforts to locate a copy of the photo, no one has been able to produce the original, though at least twenty people, including Ivan Sanderson, as well as *Mothman Prophecies* author John Keel have claimed to have seen it with their own eyes. If it indeed exists, the genuine article may be one day be found in an issue of *Saga Magazine* circa 1965 to 1967, according to Richard Freeman's research.

The most famous flying monster in American lore is probably the Jersey Devil. A resident of southern New Jersey's desolate Pine Barrens, the Jersey Devil seems to combine elements of different legendary animals, as well as a local legend about a curse with alleged ties to witchcraft. Though a real estate hoax may have been behind the Devil's origin, a flurry of documented sightings during the Jersey Devil's heyday in January, 1909 are worth examining. The most famous report, made by Mr. and Mrs. Nelson Evans of Gloucester on January 19th, includes some intriguing details. After observing the animal on the roof of their shed for about ten minutes, the couple claimed that the Jersey Devil was three and a half feet tall, with a head like a dog or horse set atop a long neck. They also noticed that the animal had two-foot wings, a long tail and long, gangly legs. An illustration based on the Nelson's description appeared in the *Philadelphia Evening Bulletin,* along with their story. The drawing at first seems quite absurd, unless we compare some of its characteristics to that of the rhamphorhynchoids.

One might expect that encounters with so called flying dragons would have faded by the start of the 20th century, at a time when rapid advancements in industry seemed to propel us into a new era. It was an age in which humans began to develop an extreme God complex. However, in the last chapter, we showed that living pterosaur accounts have been coming out of places like Africa and Oceania even in the last few decades. But, how are we to address the multitude of modern pterosaur reports that have emerged all over the North American continent in recent years?

Explorer Bill Gibbons, who frequently lectures about the *ropen* and living dinosaurs, heard of a pterosaur encounter by an outdoorsman named John Morgan in northeast Utah during 1956 or 1957. Mr. Morgan's son had approached Gibbons after his lecture, and had explained how his father had come upon the pterosaur while out hiking, causing the unusual animal to fly away. During the early 1960s, a couple motoring through northern California's Trinity National Forest supposedly spotted the silhouette of a giant bird flying overhead. The couple estimated that the bird's wingspan was fourteen feet across, and later they described the thing as looking like a pterodactyl.

On the opposite coast, a New York businessman claimed he was piloting his private plane over the Hudson River in May of 1961, when he was threatened by a *"damned big bird, bigger than an eagle."* The pilot later explained, *"For a moment I doubted my sanity because it looked more like a pterodactyl out of the prehistoric ages."* The pilot also noted that the animal resembled *"a fighter plane making a pass, with scarcely a movement of its wings."*

My thanks to the Gulf Coast Bigfoot Research Organization for forwarding the following report to me. It apparently took place during the latter part of 1964 in the piney woods of east Texas. A man who wanted to keep his identity anonymous wrote, *"This unusual sighting occurred when I was about 15 years of age. I was on Thanksgiving break from school, out snake hunting along Pine Island Bayou. I was standing along the bank of the bayou facing north when I looked up and to my right (east) only to see, at a distance of roughly 100 yards away, a positively huge bird flying from south to north. It was approximately flying at a height of 150 feet and I was able to observe its flight for a total of one minute or so before it disappeared into a cloud bank."* The witness goes on to describe the creature as, *"A light plum colour, normally feathered, wingspan estimated at 10-20 feet (bigger, longer than anything I've ever seen on any living, known bird) greyish clawed feet and greyish beak. In profile it resembled a pterodactyl more so than any bird I am familiar with either in movies, pictures, real life or drawings of same. Its wings moved methodically with an economy of motion which barely seemed fluid enough to support its weight or keep it in motion, let alone airborne. Its wings when spread, had an almost skeletal semi-transparency about them."*

Pine Island Bayou happens to be in Hardin County, in the heart of the Big Thicket. As I mentioned in chapter one, this remote area in southeast Texas has a rich history of Bigfoot sightings. The first native people in the area, who found parts of it to be litreally impenetrable, appropriately named the Thicket. It is a massive network of swampy, dense forests that covers more than 12,000 square miles. On my first Bigfoot expedition there in September of 2002, I discovered an unusual, large three-toed track, which I made a plaster cast of. All those who studied the cast agreed that the track seemed to have a bird-like quality. After one expert proclaimed the track to be from an escaped emu, (the tall, flightless relative of the ostrich), I discarded the cast. In retrospect, I wish that I had kept it!

The next accounts come from Ohio, which like Texas seems to produce a proportionately high number of these reports. Ron Schaffner, one of Ohio's leading cryptozoologists writes that, "During the summer of 1967 near Middletown, Ohio a huge bird was sighted flying over several

Modern sightings of pterosaurs have been reported all over North America

farms. Mr. James Morgan told me that the creature had a wingspan from about 15-20 feet and was dark in colour. His description was that of a pterodactyl. Four other witnesses saw the bird as it glided over their porch."

Tennessee Bigfoot lady Mary Green received a report from a nameless person who informed her of another Ohio incident, this time from North Ridgeville in Lorain County during 1968 or 1969. The witness wrote, *"I too, saw pterodactyl like creatures flying high in the sky. I was only a small child, so of course when I tried to tell anyone of what I saw it was all chalked up to my large imagination. But I know and swear to this day that they looked just like what I now know are...pterodactyls. They were very large. I almost thought they were small planes. After they began to get closer, I hid down low under some bushes. There were about 7, maybe 9 of them flying over. I believe them to be flying north. They were all skin, no feathers at all and they were very quiet. I had recently seen a program about thunderbirds and wondered if this could have been what I saw. But these absolutely had no feathers and had wings like bats."* Mary Green adds that she has spoken with another eyewitness, who claimed to have had a similar sighting in Montgomery County, Ohio during 1950 or 1951.

Still in the Midwest, there is a vivid account from the town of Park Forest, Illinois. Again, an anonymous person writes, *"I, along with four of my friends, saw a pteranodon about three to four feet tall around April of 1969. I was like 17 or 18 years old. We were on a gravel road riding in my friend's Mustang on a road south of Park Forest. My friend leaned up over the steering wheel and stared at an angle out of the windshield. I asked him what he was doing and he didn't answer me. He just kept staring out the windshield, so I leaned forward and looked up and silhouetted against the full moon, sitting on the top of a telephone pole was this pteranodon."* The description goes on, *"The body was covered with fur like a bat. It had wings folded up tight against its sides and you could see little claws at the end of each folded wing. It had a tail similar in length to that of a cat, but it was smooth like a rat's tail, except for a single tuft of hair at the end. The neck and head were smooth leather like, no hair at all. The whole time it was switching its tail around like a cat does when they are aggravated. It eventually looked down at us in the car and threw its head back, opened its mouth, showing some very impressive teeth and let out a blood-curdling screech. With three flaps of its wings sailed silently toward a large marsh south of our position and disappeared into the fog."*

Nick Sucik has collected a pterosaur report from a man named Robert F., who claimed that he spotted a creature at Lake Dewey in the Sisters Lakes Region of Michigan during July, 1969. According to Robert, the sky had suddenly gone black when he and his fishing companion looked up and saw an enormous, leathery looking-bird that only flapped its wings twice, while crossing the tiny lake.

From a creationist website comes a detailed account from a marine named Eskin Kuhn, who claimed that he was stationed at Guantanamo Bay, Cuba in July of 1971. Kuhn writes, *"I saw 2 Pterosaurs flying together at low altitude, very close in range from where I was standing, so that I had a perfectly clear view of them. The structure and the texture of the wings appeared to be very similar to that of bats; particularly in that the struts of the wings emanated from a "hand" as fingers would; except that a couple of the fingers were short and the other ran out to the tip of the wing, others back to the trailing edge of the wing to stretch the wing membrane as a kite would. The Pterosaurs I saw had the short hind legs attached to the rearwordmost part of the wing, and they had a long tail trailing behind with a tuft of hair at the end. The head was disproportionately large, with a long crest at the back, long bill, long neck with a crook in it. The vertebrae of their backs was noticeable, mostly between the shoulders. I would estimate their wingspan to be roughly 10 feet."* Kuhn, who claims to be an artist with a sharp eye for detail, drew a sketch of the two animals, with the result being astonishingly similar to eyewitness Richard Guzman's illustration.

Ropen researcher Paul Nation has collected a pterosaur report from a Colorado rancher named Ron Monteleone. The incident actually occurred just across the border in northern New Mexico during June of 1972. According to Monteleone, he was travelling south in his truck along I-25 near Maxwell, when he spotted a huge, flying creature coming up out of an arroyo or gulley. He quickly brought his truck to a complete stop, and watched the unusual animal fly across the interstate, and down into another arroyo, eventually disappearing in a southerly direction. An experienced hang-glider, Ron estimated that the creature's wingspan was easily twenty-five to thirty feet across. He did not notice if there was a tail, but the creature's long legs hanging out behind stuck in his memory. Years later, Ron recognized his quarry as he watched a segment from the movie *Jurassic Park 3*. The segment in the film featured animated pterodactyls.

Continuing in the western United States, there are numerous reports from Multnomah County, Oregon during the mid 1970s. In one case, four youths were walking down their street in a wooded area one afternoon when they came upon what seemed to be a giant bird. As one youth described it, *"I would guess the wingspan was about 20 feet or so. Back then I thought it was a lot bigger. It was medium brown in colour, had webbed feet, long tail, webbed wings. I would guess its beak or mouth was about 2 ½ to 3 feet long. It didn't appear to have any feathers on it, looked kind of leathery. It appeared to be a pterodactyl, from what I had seen in books. When it was flying around it had, what appeared to be a large snake or something in its mouth. We were all scared that it might come back and get us, so we all ran to my house. We told my mom and she thought we were nuts, so we didn't tell a lot of other people after that."*

The eyewitness continues, *"After a few years, we started hearing about more people who had seen a pterodactyl. One of them was a friend of my mom's. Her mother had found one in their backyard. She said it looked sick. She didn't want to take a picture of it or call anyone, for fear they would capture and probably harm the creature. She and her daughter just watched it for a couple of days until it flew away."* Another female eyewitness claimed she saw a pterosaur defecate in the bed of her father's pickup truck as the creature flew over their house. In addition, another Oregon resident approached Bill Gibbons and confided how she had stepped outside one day, and was shocked to see a giant bird with a monkey-like face, and twenty-five foot wingspan, perched on the side of her house. The woman explained to Gibbons that as she watched, the creature launched itself and flew away.

In chapter two, we recounted the numerous events that transpired in southern Texas during the Bicentennial Year (1976). Indeed, sightings in that region seem to have continued up until the present. Around certain other parts of the United States, chance encounters with our flying phantoms were occurring as well. In northern Pennsylvania, which has a rich tradition of so-called thunderbird reports, there is an account from Tuscarora Mountain circa 1981. On August 08th at 9:30 in the morning, Darlene and Laverne Alford were driving on Highway 74 toward Icksburg, when supposedly two large birds that were standing in the road took off in front of them. For about fifteen minutes or so, the couple was able to observe the two creatures as they flew away. Apparently, the animals stood three feet tall, with a wingspan close to fifteen feet across. Leverne also noticed that they seemed to have bony crests on the tops of their heads. One of them later commented, *"They didn't seem to have any feathers. They looked like they were covered in skin. They were dark grey in colour. I immediately thought of those prehistoric birds."*

Jonathan Whitcomb provides us with the next account, which he received through his *Living Pterosaurs* website. To me, the description sounds strikingly similar to Richard Guzman's. The eyewitness - a young man named Shawn from Texarkana, Arkansas - writes about sitting with his older brother in their carport back during 1982. He writes, *"It was getting dark but there was plenty of light in the sky when we saw what we believe to be a pterodactyl. The wingspan seemed to be about 25 to 30 feet wide. It was probably about 70 to 80 feet off the ground, flying over a large tree in front of the house. I never saw the wings flap, it just glided on air. The incident was very brief, but none the less was an awesome sight to see. If someone would have told me that they had seen a creature like that, I doubt I would have believed the story until I saw it for my-self."* Shawn continues, *"We saw the creature for approximately 20 seconds. We did not see any signs of feathers, just sharp-edged wings, the sharp, pointed beak and the sharp, pointed crest on its head. We did not see any tail. I have looked at my dinosaur book and the picture of the pter-anodon looks like what I saw."*

Returning to the west coast, there is yet another contribution from Ron Schaffner. From Thermal, California there is a second-hand account from the friend of a female graduate who writes, *"My closest friend has seen a creature (along with her sister). It happened in Thermal, California in 1983. Duke (Doberman Pincher) was tied to a leash, barking violently. They let him go, thinking it was a coyote or rabbit. The dog ran around the house, but stopped short and continued to bark. Both my friend and her sister ran toward the dog and in front of them stood a 6-foot winged, featherless creature. The body was very muscular, like a man. But the skin was leathery like an elephant. It had long nails at the end of its toes. The head was the shape of a pterodactyl with red bulging eyes and protruding bone in the front and back of its head. It turned and looked at my friend and her sister and crouched down, tucked its wings and flew off. The wings were so big you could hear them flap in the wind as it flew away. The dog chased it till he lost sight of it."*

The years 1982 and 1983 seem to be significant, when we consider that Richard Guzman, James Thompson, and others, *all* had sightings during that span. Yet another report from that era found its way to me after a lecture on `Big Bird`, though the animal in question may be of the feathered variety! A man named Russell, along with two friends who I am told are now police officers, apparently were camping near Hondo, Texas during 1982. Their friend Michael DuPree writes, *"They had already settled in for the night and I believe it was around one or two in the morning when they were awakened by a loud swooshing noise and upon investigating in a hurry, they claim to have seen an oversized bird of some kind that had feathers. It was trying to land in the trees above where they were camping. The trees were real thick and they were trying to grab their guns and get out of the canopy to have a better look, but it was overcast and by then they had got out into the open. He said they could only make out the outline of an oversized, enormous bird heading toward one of the hilltops surrounding their place. One of the guys went into the camp to get a flashlight to try and see where it landed and when they spotted it, all they could make out in the faint light was an outline of the biggest bird with feathers they had ever seen."* One of the men was apparently so frightened, that he high-tailed it back to Houston in the middle of the night.

It appears as though Texas is a hotspot for flying creature reports, as is the Midwest and in particular the state of Ohio. Case in point our next encounter, which - once again - arrives courtesy of the `Gulf Coast Bigfoot Research Organization` database. A correspondent from Columbianna wrote that he was out walking one afternoon in the mid 1980s (possibly 1985) near a junkyard. Suddenly the witness looked up and noticed, *"Exactly what I had seen in books about prehistoric animals. I just thought, That's a pterodactyl*! and ran back to the house fast." The description continues, *"It had a long neck, leathery skin and the skin flap wings with claws extending from the wing. It was sort of a reddish, brown grey in colour. It might have had feathers, but I didn't get that long of a look. The legs stuck straight out behind it. It was very high in the sky and still very large."* According to the witness, the previous night some unseen assailant had swooped down, creating a *"very large gust of air,"* which caused his cousin to scream and fall down.

A widely published account from the Midwest is the Brookfield, Wisconsin, thunderbird story, as reported by Allison Jornlin. According to the witness, the sighting occurred on the afternoon of September 21, 1988 in Brookfield, a suburb of Milwaukee. A twenty-five year old man named Kevin W. claimed he was staring out the window of Elmbrook Memorial Hospital, when he noticed a dark figure moving among the clouds. At first he thought it might be a small aeroplane, which would have been flying dangerously low in his opinion. In an instant though, Kevin was startled when he realized that the object resembled a bird, *"Bigger than a full-size pickup truck"* He estimated its total length to be between twelve to fifteen feet, the same as its wingspan. The creature seemed to glide on air currents without flapping its wings, and flew within a hundred yards of his window. Kevin claimed that the monster even turned and looked at him, *"At some point, I was aware that it was aware of me,"* he recalled. He described the head as being pointy, and aerodynamic, and remarked, *"I couldn't make out any feathers. It was more bat-like."* Kevin seemed convinced that what he observed that day, as weird and inconceivable as it seemed, was in fact a pterodactyl. Jornlin's thoughtful article addresses the incident's psychological impact on Kevin, after he witnesses something that forces him to question his own sanity.

From the city of Middletown, Ohio, which hosted a rash of pterosaur sightings in 1967, comes a more recent report from sometime in the early 1990s. The information arrives via the GCBRO database, second hand. Supposedly, a group of seventeen year olds were prowling around an old barn outside Middletown, when, *"They saw a large, featherless bird about six feet, four inches tall. Its skin appeared like leather. As they entered the barn, the bird turned to look at them, moving only its head."* Understandably, the group of youths fled the scene in terror.

Ron Schaffner, who has already done much to further our knowledge of pterodactyl reports in the Midwest and elsewhere, published a sighting that occurred around Thanksgiving of 1993. The location was near Orin, Wyoming, which falls in line with other Rocky Mountain accounts from states like Utah and New Mexico. A woman wrote Schaffner, explaining how she and her husband were on their way from Sheridan, Wyoming, to Chadron, Nebraska, to pick up his children from his ex-wife. The couple had pulled off I-25 at a rest stop, and just as they re-entered the freeway, they noticed a large animal standing in a field. They were both intrigued, so they pulled off in order to observe the creature. The wife wrote, *"It stood – my estimate is about five feet tall, husband estimates six feet. It was greenish grey and appeared to be a pterodactyl. We sat by the side of the road for about twenty minutes watching this thing. It sat and flexed and stretched its wings, each of which were as long as its body was tall. We stayed as long as we could and we did stop again on our return trip, but the thing was gone."* Upon further questioning by Schaffner, the couple revealed the following, *"The head and beak were not delicate in any way, more like that of a horse. The wing looked thick, leathery bat-like wings, but not exactly like those of a bat. The skin of the animal was thick and leathery, no feathers. The torso and legs were thick and powerful. The one we saw didn't have such a big horn on the back of its head."*

A nightmarish winged apparition confronted eighteen-year-old Brian Canfield of Buckley, Washington during 1994, according to an April 24th story that appeared in the *Tacoma News Tribune.* As the story goes, Brian was driving towards a settlement named Camp One at around 9:30 one evening, when the engine of his pick-up truck suddenly died as a nine foot tall figure descended from above. Jon Downes writes in *The Owlman & Others*, *"It had blue tinted fur, yellowish eyes, the feet of a bird, tufted ears and sharp straight teeth. Its wings were folded and attached to its back and broad shoulders."* Brian later stated that, *"I was scared. It raised the hair on me. The eyes were yellow, with pupils like a half moon. The mouth was pretty big. The teeth were like a wolf."* The newspaper gave the strange creature the clever name `Batsquatch` and reported that Canfield did not drink or use drugs. There is apparently a second, somewhat dubious `Batsquatch` report from a mountain climber named Butch Whitaker.

Moving on to Henderson, near Smith Mills, Kentucky, in 2001, we have our first sighting of the 21st century. A couple reportedly was driving through some wooded bottomlands near the Ohio River at midday, surveying some damage that a tornado had caused two days prior. Suddenly, they both observed, *"A giant, pterodactyl type bird."* The man described the animal as being, *"A solid red colour with smooth, leathery skin. It had no feathers, but it did have a long, curled up tail. It had a thick beak, with a knob or protrusion of some type on the top of the head. Its wingspan was at least twenty feet or better. It was so big that my wife mistook it for an aeroplane at first. The creature banked right just above the tree-tops, still descending with feet outstretched as if to land. Its feet were like those of a normal type bird with long talons. I noticed hair about five or six inches long growing just above its feet."*

Continuing our reports from the Midwest, we have an encounter by an eyewitness named Fisher Stevenson of Camden, Minnesota, during October of 2001. A huge, winged monster apparently flew close to the telephone lines near the roof of Stevenson's home. He later described the creature as looking grey, with a twenty-four foot wingspan. Fisher claimed that he could see light passing through the animal's membranous wings. Later that winter, he claimed to have another sighting.

An anonymous eyewitness from Colorado wrote how he, *"Observed what could only be what is called a pteranodon, soaring in the sky above Morgenson ponds near Mesa, Colorado. The creature had an approximate wingspan of six feet, dwarfing two eagles nearby, and had a dull tan colour skin. It had a large toothless beak, a bony head with sunken eyes, featherless body, and a pointed appendage extending from the back of the head. The leathery wings were semi-clear as I could see some light glow through. Its head turned only with the creature's course of flight and rarely flapped its wings. When the wings did move the motion seemed similar to that of a bat. I failed to see any form of tail, however I do recount seeing a full, pelican-like throat and small protrusions from the forward mid section of the wings. Whatever the thing was, it did seem to fly like a bird of prey, possessed some anatomical similarities to a pelican, the colour and wing mo-*

tions of a fruit bat, and a head protrusion similar but different from a blue heron." This alleged encounter took place on July 14th of 2004 at 2:30pm.

Over the last few years, North American pterosaur reports have continued to pop up on the Internet, due to the proliferation of paranormal websites where participants are encouraged to share their own experiences. One such report was posted by a Georgia resident named Drew Dixon, who was near a shallow creek, along with a friend during October 19th 2002. Dixon claimed they saw *"an enormous grey bird"* perched on a tree limb. The bird had leathery wings with a ten-foot span, according to Drew. Kevin Meixner of Brampton Ontario shared how he was driving to work on the morning of November 1st, 2004, when he observed, *"A strange bird-like creature."* Kevin's description is as follows, *"It looked exactly like a miniature pterodactyl like you see in the movies like Jurassic Park or on the Flintstones cartoons. The only difference is that it was much smaller, having a wingspan of about four feet. It was grey and did not appear to have any feathers. The wings were an odd shape and flapped much differently than any kind of bird I've seen flying, they looked fleshy like bat wings. It had a long, skinny, pointed tail extended straight behind it that had sort of a diamond shape at the tip."*

From the very popular cryptozoology.com website, comes what at the time of going-to-press is the most recent U.S. sighting, as reported by two young men in Zionsville, Indiana. Sam Motter and his friend Alex, both claim that in early 2006, they witnessed a pterosaur fly through their neighbourhood. Sam wrote that, *"The shape was a small body with triangular wings possessing no feathers flapping on either side. To the back of the small elongated-lemon shaped body was a proportionately long, straight tail with a swelling at the end shaped, again, somewhat like a lemon."* Upon comparing notes, the two youths concluded that the creature most resembled the species rhamphorhynchus. I managed to contact Sam, who seemed pleased that I had taken an interest in his report.

The most compelling sighting in recent years may involve a Mexican police officer in 2004. Jorge Contreras of the Santa Catarina police was patrolling with two other officers on the evening of January 13th, when they spotted a bulky, seven foot, dark grey figure, with bat-like wings standing in the middle of a soccer field. As the officers watched, the figure took off, and flew away. This is the most compelling, because a mere two hundred miles to the east of Santa Catarina, lies the sleepy Texas border town of San Benito, home of the creature known as the `Big Bird`.

Chapter 6

- Theories and Speculation -

There is still one very important question that remains to be answered, of course. What is the `Big Bird`? Perhaps cryptozoologist and author Mark Hall put it best when he wrote me, *"There is no cryptid known as `Big Bird`, just as there is no Jersey Devil and no Skunk Ape. These are all local catch-all categories that mean different things to different people."* While I agree with his statement to the extent that I believe numerous circumstances were in play once the initial hysteria had ensued, I tend to believe that a few of the more dramatic encounters may have involved an exceptionally rare and remarkable animal. Consider, for example, the cases of ambulance driver James Thompson, and the three school teachers from San Antonio, as well as that of electrician Richard Guzman. Richard, in particular, is the only eyewitness that I have interviewed personally, so I must put the most weight behind what he told me first hand. Each of these three cases involved focused, daytime, observations which lasted at least fifteen seconds. All five, seemingly ordinary, people were convinced that they had seen living pterosaurs; flying reptiles believed to be extinct for sixty-four million years.

It is at this point that we must address the pterodactyl mimics, which are in fact common birds, which are capable of displaying vaguely reptilian qualities when viewed in the proper circumstances. The degree of similarity between these imposters, and actual pterosaurs is a matter of subjective opinion, and it is this point that I take issue with. Foremost there are a number of large, primarily aquatic, birds such as pelicans, storks, herons, and cranes, which can possess impressive wingspans from seven to nine feet across. While in flight and especially at a distance, these birds can all exhibit prehistoric characteristics. Storks for example, often sport bald, leathery, heads. Pelicans possess prominent s-shaped pouches under their long, thick beaks, which resemble protruding breastbones. Pelicans, and their smaller relatives the frigate birds, also possess sharp, angular wings. Indeed, when viewing certain long-legged birds in flight, their outstretched legs somewhat resemble a tail.

The problem with simply stating the case closed at this juncture, is that most people are familiar with all of these fairly common species of birds, which can often be found near water. While their heights can be quite impressive at a close range, storks, cranes, and even herons, are easily identifiable by the average observer as nothing out of the ordinary. This is particularly the case in southern Texas, where thousands of bird species make their home, and residents spend much of their time outdoors working, fishing, and hunting. Most of the tall bird species generally sport long, thin, legs required for wading, as well as limber necks necessary for plucking prey out of the water. In essence, these types of birds are graceful in movement, and delicate in structure, despite their imposing heights and wingspans. These characteristics do not match with the `Big Bird` descriptions.

The exception may be pelicans, which have squat legs and stout bodies. Pelicans are definitely intimidating birds at close range, and the really big ones can possess a ten foot wingspan. A fifteen foot wingspan on a pelican however, is undocumented. Also, pelicans are for the most part coastal birds that do not usually stray inland, where many Big Bird sightings have been reported. If any eyewitnesses did in fact see an oversized pelican, it was perhaps San Benito police officers Gavan and Padilla, who might have overestimated the animal's size in the dim, dawn light. However, Galvan later stated that he was an avid hunter and outdoorsman, so it seems that he would have been experienced at viewing wildlife in a variety of situations.

As I mentioned in chapter four, Loren Coleman investigated pterodactyl reports coming out of Mexico's Yucatan Peninsula in his book *Curious Encounters,* and concluded that high flying frigate birds may have been mistaken for pterosaurs on occasion. During an excursion to Belize in 2004, I spent more than a few lazy days lying on the Caribbean beaches, and I found myself observing pelicans, as well as frigate birds, on an almost constant basis. At no distance did I ever mistake them for anything other than what they were. Thus, I have a difficult time accepting the notion that people could be so easily mistaken.

Other native birds that bear some consideration as `Big Bird` candidates, include the raptors such as vultures, eagles, and owls. Of these, vultures are the most promising, since they tend to have a creepy, prehistoric look, and appear quite large and menacing at close range. However, their wingspan usually tops out at about seven feet, and there is no way a vulture standing on the ground could ever be mistaken for being man-sized. More importantly, vultures are extremely common in Texas, with both turkey (*Cathartes aura*) and black vultures *(Coragyps atratus)* being regularly seen, hovering above the abundant road kill, even in major metropolitan areas.

There are some native species of eagles, which can possess wingspans around seven feet, but they are also common throughout Texas, and they sport small, hooked, beaks which make them easily identifiable to most people. Owl's beaks are generally even smaller and their wingspans top off around five feet, but they do possess the large eyes that `Big Bird` witnesses have often mentioned. But again, owls are also very familiar to most people who live in Texas. It is true that a large owl can definitely startle a person at night,when it suddenly unfurls its wings and takes off. However, to accept that any of these common birds could be built into `Big Bird` status, regardless of the circumstances, is not sufficient in my view. I regret that the sceptics are at ease with the position that the observers are not capable of identifying what animals they are in fact observing.

If we reasonably eliminate all of Texas' known species as `Big Bird` candidates, what about a specimen that has been somehow displaced? A few very large and strange, birds have been suggested as being behind the reports, including the old world hornbills (family Bucerotidae), shoebill (*Balaeniceps rex*), and marabou stork *(Leptoptilos crumeniferus)*. Hornbills display an ornate head colouration that most certainly would have been identified at some point. The bizarre looking shoebill is certainly very prehistoric in appearance, except that it is obviously feathered. Shoebills are native to the swamps where Africa's *kongamato* has been reported, but to argue that a shoebill resembles a pterosaur requires a great stretch of the imagination. The marabou stork has some similarity to Texas' wood stork, (*Mycteria americana*) but is even larger. The bottom line is that none of these birds really match the descriptions.

In fact, if I were to give consideration to any out-of-place bird, it would only be the vulture's large cousin the condor. Condors are the biggest known birds capable of flight. Their wingspans range can from nine feet across on the California species to ten or possibly eleven feet on the Andean type. Both kinds are large enough to really frighten someone who has never seen one at close range. Though they don't stand quite as tall as a man, condors *do* somewhat match some of the Big Bird descriptions, particularly the sighting by Jackie Davies and Tracy Lawson.

Both of the known condor species are endangered. The range of the California species extends into Arizona's Grand Canyon, but no further east that we know of. That isn't to say that there couldn't be an unknown species native to the remote mountains of northern Mexico. Jon Downes has pointed out that it would make perfect sense for condors to have inhabited Mexico at some point, since it would connect the two known species geographically. Also, we can't rule out the possibility that one of the Grand Canyon specimens may have strayed out of its normal territory. The problem with this theory is that the lower Rio Grande Valley surely ranks among the flattest places on Earth. It's not at all the type of habitat where a mountain dwelling Condor would care to linger for any extended period.

A more tantalizing possibility is that `Big Bird` could be a species unrecognized by science; possibly the giant, supposedly extinct, relatives of condors and vultures known as teratorns. [11] These massive raptors were alive and well in the Americas up until 6,000 years ago, according to the multitude of fossils that have been found in the La Brea tar pits. The largest teratorn specimen, *Argentivas magnificens* of South America, boasted an aeroplane sized, twenty-seven foot wingspan, making it the largest, known flying bird that ever lived. The teratorns are presumed to have gone extinct with other oversized megafauna at the end of the Ice Age. Obviously, if we could confirm that some of these massive birds had managed to survive into the present times, and then appeared before our slack-jawed eyewitnesses in south Texas, the `Big Bird` mystery could be put to rest. There are numerous reports of giant, vulture-like birds, which stem from places like Alaska, Pennsylvania and Illinois that support this theory.

The most famous incident involved a nine-year-old boy named Marlon Lowe of Lawndale, Illinois, during November of 1977. In plain sight of several witnesses including his mother, Marlon was apparently plucked off the ground by one of two giant, black vulture-like birds that swooped down from above. As the onlookers watched in horror, Marlon was carried several feet by the predatory bird, as he struggled to free himself from a horrible fate. Eventually, the bird let go and Marlon fell safely to the ground. In the weeks that followed, reports of giant birds emanated from other parts of central Illinois. There is even a film shot bat Lake Shelbyville by a man named "Texas" John Huffer which shows two, fairly large, birds taking off and flying away. While some have dismissed the film as showing only vultures, I have viewed it numerous times and feel that the subject's wingspans do seem unusually large when compared to the surrounding trees.

There are a number of other clues, which suggest a massive, raptor like bird like the teratorn could still exist. For example, there are numerous Native American legends about eagle-like thunderbirds, perhaps named because of the thunderous beating of their mighty wings, although there could be a link to the wind currents associated with storm fronts. Irregardless, the thunderbirds were regarded as real animals, basically resembling an Eagle, but capable of eclipsing the sun. Some legends tell of thunderbirds carrying off children or other unfortunate victims, presumably as a meal. The name itself remains awe inspiring, as evidenced by its use from a car manufacturer, as well as makers of cheap but potent wine. The name has also been linked to the famous `Thunderbird Photo`, which purports to show an enormous pterosaur outstretched against a barn, demonstrating how people are conditioned to label any large, winged animal a bird.

An enormous bird attempted to abduct Marlon Lowe of Lawndale, Illinois

So, there is a real possibility that some teratorns do await rediscovery on some remote mountaintop. The problem is that several `Big Bird` witnesses took the time to look through textbooks in order to figure out what it was precisely that they had seen. In several cases, what these eyewitnesses are describing does not match at all with the teratorns, or any birds really. Could the name `Big Bird` really be a misnomer?

One very important detail when dealing with all of these reports is the absence of feathers that is described by eyewitnesses, often referred to as "leathery skin". We now think that some pterosaurs may have possessed proto-feathers, a kind of light, fluffy coating similar to fur, but there is no evidence they were fully feathered like modern birds. Therefore, the specific descriptions of smooth, bare, skin by `Big Bird` witnesses is significant in establishing that we are probably not dealing with any type of bird. The presence of feathers on virtually all birds is usually quite obvious, with the exception of some bald-headed birds like storks, vultures, and turkeys. By design, birds are dependant on their feathers in order to fly, and maintain the proper body temperature.

There is another bold theory that has been proposed by the lineage of cryptozoologists that includes Bernard Heuvelmans, Ivan Sanderson, Mark Hall and Loren Coleman. All of these researchers are convinced that lurking somewhere out there is an undiscovered species of giant bat. As discussed in chapter four, there are legends and reports from the jungles of Indo China and Africa that suggest such an animal may exist. However, in regards to sightings in the Americas, there is a problem.

There are two major suborders of bats, the often robust megachiroptera of the Old World which includes the herbivorous fruit bats and flying foxes, as well as the primarily insect-eating microchiroptera, which have a worldwide distribution. As far as we know, there are no representatives of megachiroptera in the Americas, and there's no evidence of a large, microchiroptera species in existence anywhere. In fact, no truly gigantic bat has ever been unearthed, even though bat fossils are fairly common in caves. The largest known bats, the flying foxes of Asia and Indonesia, possess wingspans over seven feet wide, but they only weigh about two and half pounds. In contrast, the largest known bat in the Americas possesses a wingspan barely nine inches across. If we consider the various behaviours that have been attributed to `Big Bird`, as well as the *ropen* and *kongamato*, they do not in any way match what we would expect of a bat. For example, the apparent attacks on humans, which have been widely reported, are not typical of large bats, which unless provoked, are basically harmless to humans. Unless perhaps we are dealing with some type of enormous vampire bat, a terrifying notion indeed!

Unlike our `Big Bird`, bats typically do not spend much time on the ground, nor are they exceptional gliders; a characteristic that has come up repeatedly. In fact, the `bat word` has only really been used in reference to `Big Bird's` wings, although it's true that on a few occasions the face has been described as looking cat-like, monkey-like or lacking a beak. On the other hand, the words `pteranodon`, `pterodactyl` and `pterosaur` come up repeatedly, especially when people look to books for answers. In light of *tacuache* translating to "possum," the giant bat theory bears some consideration; since a large bat might somewhat resemble a flying possum. However, it could also be a reference to the animal having a mouth full of sharp, little teeth, a pterosaur characteristic. Besides, in the last chapter we mentioned the flat-faced pterosaur species that has been named `batrachagnathus`, due to its bat-like resemblance.
Another radical proposal that has been put forward by author Mark Hall has not been specifically

linked to Big Bird, but it may bear consideration when speculating about flying things of a gigantic nature. Hall believes that a giant owl, which he affectionately calls `Bighoot`, may be responsible for some reports of winged monsters. There are already some pretty sizeable owls in North America, which possess a five-foot wingspan, but Big Hoot is purported to be man-sized or taller. Corroboration of this cryptid comes to me in the form of an e-mail from a Florida woman. She wrote me that her father, a truck driver, once had to pull his rig over while traversing the everglades expressway known as `Alligator Alley`, due to an enormous owl blocking the road.

Hall has suggested `Bighoot` as a possible explanation for accounts of the `Owlman`, a nightmarish, winged humanoid that has been encountered by several young people in southern England. Jon Downes, author of *The Owlman & Others*, once told me that he has a great deal of respect for Mark Hall, but that something about the giant owl theory didn't sit right with him. Loren Coleman has confirmed that `Bighoot` might explain some of the reports of West Virginia's `Mothman`. It is paramount to note that there are parallels in all of these winged monster cases, when you consider that people have attempted to link the `Mothman`, `Owlman` and even `Big Bird` with paranormal phenomena such as witchcraft, livestock mutilations, U.F.O.s and even Men in Black.

There is no denying that these types of winged creature waves bear similarities. Accounts of apparently winged humanoids have also gotten into the mix. One somewhat famous incident, which occurred in Houston's historic Heights neighbourhood during the early morning hours of June 18, 1953, involves an entity that has become known as the Batman. According to the newspaper article, Hilda Walker, Howard Phillips, and Judy Meyers, were sitting on the porch outside their apartment building when suddenly, a huge shadow passed over their heads, landing in a nearby pecan tree. To their surprise, the shadow appeared to resemble a tall man donning a kind of paratrooper uniform, but with bat-like wings attached. The entity seemed to be encased in a grey halo of light, which faded out slowly as the mysterious figure vanished in front of their startled eyes. An acquaintance of mine in Houston has brought another possible Batman encounter to my attention.

Now admittedly, as a cryptozoologist I prefer to concentrate on the aspects of the `Big Bird` mystery that point to an elusive and unrecognised animal species. However, in light of some of these occurrences, I suppose we must open our minds to the idea that these events really are linked to the paranormal in some way. We should consider the possibility that these entities are, in fact, visitors from a plane of existence beyond our comprehension, somehow stepping through doors that aren't usually open. This idea was first introduced by the great Charles Fort, and later explored by authors such as John Keel and later Ted Holiday in his book *The Goblin Universe*. There are numerous theories in this regard. For those who are spiritual, these apparitions are witches, dark angels, or demons, determined to divert our focus from the path of righteousness. For others, these entities represent ghosts, time travellers, or extraterrestrials with a purpose beyond our grasp. I prefer to think that there are dimensions to space and time that we do not fully understand. That being said, I still tend to lean toward more earthly explanations.

It does seem that all indications point to `Big Bird` being a flesh and blood animal, as opposed to trickery or some sort of mechanism, unless we again choose to consider extraterrestrial origins. An unappealing notion that must be considered, is the possibility that some people are simply fabricating these reports; perpetuating a massive hoax. Unfortunately, in some instances this is

Like West Virginia's Mothman, Big Bird may be linked to UFOs

the case, as investigators are often confronted with the occasional oddball who is hoping to get their name in print, or perhaps even discredit the investigators. But, to propose that such a wide cross section of apparently normal people would waste their time on something so dubious, doesn't make any sense to me. As I've stated, most witnesses who come forward with these reports are met with extreme ridicule from their peers. The gain - if any - is nominal.

Another possibility is that this is all some kind of widespread psychological phenomenon. Perhaps some people are so suggestible that they are simply hallucinating these creatures, because the desire is being planted somehow. There is a school of thought that we humans need our monsters to act as embodiments of our suppressed fears. Besides, images of pterosaurs are everywhere you look these days in movies like *Jurassic Park*, on television shows, in video games and so on. No animal embodies the mythical dragon like the pterosaurs, and dragons remain extremely significant icons in human folklore and culture worldwide. I believe there is most certainly a connection between the discovery of the Quetzacoatlus fossils in west Texas during 1975, and a few of the `Big Bird` sightings the following year.

Having touched on all the various possibilities, I return again to the pterosaurs, which tend to be my favourite `Big Bird` candidates as this body of work clearly makes evident.

True, they were not birds.
But, as the product of convergent evolution, they may have bore a striking resemblance to their modern day counterparts. We still do not know much about the pterosaurs, but the prevalent theory holds that they descended along with their cousins the dinosaurs, crocodilians, and birds, from a common reptilian ancestor. In light of recent discoveries of so-called proto feathers on some pterosaur fossils, the true relationship between the flying reptiles and modern birds is intriguing.

The earliest known pterosaurs were of the rhamphorhynchoid type, and most of those were as small as robins. They appear to have developed into the larger pterosaurs, whilst dropping the long tails. But, there is now evidence that certain rhamphorhynchoids may have possessed head crests similar to the pterosaurs, which goes against earlier beliefs. The pterosaurs appear to have been pretty much worldwide in their distribution, and they ruled the skies for at least a hundred and sixty million years, until the presumed extinction of the dinosaurs took place. Contrary to popular belief, the pterosaurs were not dinosaurs. They were unique.

If you accept the theory of evolution as fact, then any pterosaur descendants alive today would have adapted to their modern environment, meaning we are dealing with an entirely new species, unknown in the fossil record. The lack of pterosaur fossils that date less than sixty-five million years is troubling, but could represent a massive reduction in population, rather than a complete and total extinction. What's more, there are issues with the dating methods currently used by scientists. Most fossils are dated by their relationships to the geological layers in which they are found and also with so-called radium tests. Organic matter is required for accurate carbon dating, but unfortunately it has not presented itself on a pterosaur fossil yet. Irregardless, the physical evidence for continued pterosaur survival is not there.

Therefore, it appears that we are in the awkward position of relying solely on the anecdotal evidence, which comes to us in the form of eyewitness testimony and numerous legends that date

Statue representing a thunderbird located at Kempenfelt Bay, Ontario

back thousands of years. We have at least seven people that have gone on record as having seen pterosaurs alive and well in modern Texas. The eyewitnesses had a reasonable amount of time and daylight to in which to make their observations. Three teachers, as well as an ambulance driver, had identified their quarry in a book. So had sisters, Libby and Deany Ford, who had done come to the same conclusion. There are at least dozens of similar reports stemming from around North America, which suggests that the phenomenon could be real.

The majority of `Big Bird` sightings have been somewhat brief. Many have happened at night when viewing conditions are poor. Armando Grimaldo, who was as close as anyone would ever want to come to the creature, noted the absence of a beak and feathers on his attacker. Many witnesses have also described exceptionally large, red, eyes. The Ford sisters, though they had stated it was definitely a pteranodon that they had seen, had also described the animal's face as appearing somewhat bat-like. A family who had a fleeting glimpse of `Big Bird` near Olmito described the face as being monkey-like. Residents in La Palma have called the creature's face catlike. Tracey Lawson and Jackie Davies described it as gorilla-like.

As we can see, there can be different interpretations of something like `Big Bird`. Much of that, no doubt, has to do with an individual's perception and frame of reference. If odd-looking pterosaurs are flying around, people are going to process the data in different ways. Because they possess wings and elongated skulls, some people will refer to them as strange birds. Others will focus on their height, and bare, muscular, bodies, and perceive them as somewhat humanoid. Still others may notice their mouth full of teeth, and think of a cat, or even a monkey! People will draw their comparisons and conclusions based on whatever makes the most sense to them, because such animals do not fit neatly into the context of our modern world. Alverico Guajardo, who had his eyes trained on the `Big Bird` for several minutes, may have summed it up best when he remarked that the creature resembled, *"Something from another planet, like a bird, but not a bird."*

The final way of analysing the `Big Bird` descriptions is from a behavioural standpoint. This is difficult, because we don't really know much about pterosaur behaviour except what we can deduce from their fossils. It appears that many of them lived near water, and their dentition indicates that they were predators, so they presumably ate fish. Because their bones were basically hollow, pterosaurs were extremely lightweight, and therefore even the largest pterodactyls could not have easily carried off large prey. It's likely that they would have been opportunistic feeders at all times, armed with weapons like sharp claws and teeth.

In the cases of `Big Bird`, *kongamato*, and even the *ropen*, there are several accounts of creatures attacking humans. While we can't be sure if this is the type of behaviour would be typical of a pterosaur, it certainly isn't typical of any large bird or bat. Additionally, attacks on humans are mentioned in *chupacabras* reports and also in many dragon legends, so if these animals do exist, they definitely seem to act aggressively towards humans. These confrontations would in a way, insure their immortality in our legends and folklore, which is clearly what has happened.

Yet another characteristic that is often mentioned in these reports is the ability of `Big Bird` to glide almost effortlessly, without too much wing-flapping. This definitely fits with what we do know about pterosaur physiology. Because they were built so aerodynamically, pterosaurs were made to be exceptional gliders. Their unique anatomy also allowed them to move around on the ground when necessary, but the sky was clearly their domain. We must not forget that virtually all `Big Bird` reports have taken place near bodies of water. Water definitely seems to be a key component in virtually all `Big Bird` sightings, as well as the majority of the modern pterosaur reports.

In conclusion, it does not seem reasonable to presume that a group of pterosaurs would have made their home in the modern Rio Grande Valley of Texas, or other parts of the United States, given the fact that they are not seen very often. However, it does seem within reason that a group of these animals could populate remote parts of Mexico's unexplored mountains, or the marshes and jungles of Central America. There are native traditions and ancient engravings in Mexico that support the continued existence of such an animal. The late, great Dr. Richard Greenwell had a correspondent in Mexico who was convinced such a creature could be found living in his country. An elderly settler in the Yucatan told an acquaintance of mine that prehistoric animals could still be found living within its rainforests. Having spent much time in the neo-tropics, I confer that the jungles of Central or South America could conceal a small population of living pterosaurs.

For reasons unknown, these animals may periodically migrate or roam, following certain weather patterns, or perhaps striking out in search of food or to breed. Another large, winged animal, the wandering albatross, (*Diomedea exulans*), is capable of circling the world multiple times throughout the course of its life. Conceivably, these pterosaur descendants may even be capable of crossing the oceans from distant places like Africa or New Guinea. If in fact these winged marvels have continued to exist anywhere on our modern planet, we can now explain our dragons, thunderbirds, the *chupacabras*, the Jersey Devil, `Big Bird`, and countless other winged monsters that have been recorded throughout history.

As mankind continues to infringe further and further into the unexplored regions of our planet, we may at last discover the true identity of the `Big Bird`. Only one thing remains certain, an extraordinary entity passed over south Texas back in 1976, changing dozens, if not thousands of lives forever. A modern legend was born.

Appendix 1

- Pterosaur Dawn and Dusk -

by Leland Hales

It is dawn on the Niobrara Sea 85 million years ago. A strange dark silhouette sits floating on the warm sea's surface. As the sun begins to illuminate the early morning sky, the figure begins to resemble that of a sea bird of drastically different design. The first rays of direct sunlight strike the water, and this animal takes flight. We can now see the detailed features of its bat-like leathery skinned wings with no discernible feathers, stretching nearly twenty feet from tip to tip. Its long crane-like neck holds a smallish head with a toothless pointed jaw. The head is adorned with a long horn-like crest protruding from the top of the skull just above its eyes and extending back nearly half the length its body.

The creature is truly something different than bird or bat; it is a reptile in every sense of scientific description: This is called Pteranodon, and belongs to a group of flying reptiles named `pterosaurs`.

The ancient Niobrara Sea extended across North America from the Artic Ocean to the Gulf of Mexico. The shores stretched from the Rocky Mountains on the Western side of the sea, to the Eastern edge of the Dakotas, and southward to New Mexico and Texas. This effectively cut North America in half. At 200 metres deep, it was teaming with sea life that provided a perfect feeding habitat for the pterosaurs of this time.

As the pteranodon flies just above the water on powerful wings, it begins plucking the first of many fish from the surface. But below the surface is other reptilian competition. A long-necked elasmosaurus stretching over 40 feet, fishes from within the water. Using strong flippers and long tails to move swiftly, this marine reptile is fully evolved to life in the ocean. Although both held a common ancestor some 320 million years ago, now they are two utterly opposite creatures on different evolutionary paths, ironically attempting to achieve the same goal, catching fish.

Unlike the elasmosaurus, pteranodon is no stranger to land and, seeking less of a contest for food, he heads for the coast. Flying back inland, the pteranodon tests his luck finding a more terrestrial meal. He, like most animals, was probably no stranger to scavenging food, and a recently washed up carcass on some beach would provide a welcome meal. Able to cover countless miles of coastline, pteranodon stands an excellent chance of discovering newly deposited remains offered up by the falling tides. Now over land, he glides above the costal forest, watching below him the countless forms of dinosaurs playing out modern-day scenarios of life and death struggles in the wild. Herds of plant-eating animals of enormous size, and taking many different forms are grazing in open areas. Some walk on all-fours with lons tails, and short necks, eating with a cow-like posture, while others graze tree tops using long giraffe-like necks counterbalanced by even *longer* tails. Still others sit upright on large hind legs, giving a kangaroo-like appearance using their short front legs to pull tree branches forward for eating. A large two-legged toothy predator sits behind the tree line, hidden to the others, and completely undetected.

But they are all different from the pterosaurs in many ways; they are true dinosaurs. So if pteranodon is not a dinosaur, or a marine reptile, but all three are reptiles; where do pterosaurs fit in? And where did they come from?

To make the distinctions, we have to go back even further in time. The pterosaur family tree is thought to have started over 250 million years ago, with an order of early reptiles called thecodontians. This order was not overly impressive, some looking very much like a modern-day monitor lizard, or a common backyard chameleon. But a suborder of thecodonts, called ornithosuchians, may have held the common ancestor of all three. Thecodonts were only around for about 40 millions years, but somehow gave rise to a very diverse group of animals. Dinosaurs and pterosaurs branched off at approximately the same time, somewhere between 250 to 230 million years ago. The marine reptiles lineage split at the same time, but did not become fully aquatic for another 30 million years.

So if the split occurred at approximately the same geologic time, why are they not all dinosaurs?

What we have here is a clear evolutionary path by all three descendants of the same ancestor; one by land, one by sea, and one by air.

The pterosaur placed all its adaptive efforts toward the goal of flight, creating an animal that departed from its predecessors in every way for the sole purpose of flight. Not since the first insects had any other animal achieved this goal.

While the pterosaurs pursued the goal of flight, dinosaurs placed their evolutionary efforts toward becoming larger and more powerful on land. Early reptiles' body design held one problem to be solved before large size could be achieved. The answer to the problem on land is what defines a dinosaur. By placing the legs directly under the body, a greater body mass and size can be achieved with less stress on the limbs. While other reptiles hold their legs out to the sides, this poses a problem for achieving great size. The dinosaur is defined from all other reptiles, quite simply, by the hip structure. Although several thoughts exist on pterosaur's type of locomotion once on the ground, the hip-structure is different from that of the dinosaurs, thus placing them in their own special classification.

Although the hip design is the main reason that pterosaurs are not dinosaurs, the differences between it and all other animals only begin there. This is a truly extraordinary creature the world had never seen before. The pterosaurs' adaptive changes led to bone structures that have yet to be duplicated by even modern-day birds themselves. Modifications to the arm and hand structure produced an extended pinky with overstretched skin creating the wing structure. The remaining digits became tiny claws. Wings were reinforced by closely-spaced fibres called actinofibrillae. These stiffened the wings, and would have prevented a tear from running down the entire length. The bones themselves became entirely hollow and large in diameter, but thin; not unlike a cardboard tube left behind by wrapping paper. These bones have been found through analysis to be 86 times stronger than mammal bones. Nearly all muscles attached to the bones were now dedicated to the purpose of flight. This also may indicate the possibility of a warm-blooded metabolism to accommodate for large amounts of energy needed in active flight.

The direct pterosaur lineage is equally split up. In two overlapping waves of evolution, the order called pterosauria was split into two sub-orders. Pteranodon was not the first attempt at flight, and he wouldn't be the last of his kind either. The first suborder was called rhamphorynchoidea; meaning "pointy curved nose," appearing in the Triassic period (215 million years ago). Some as small as sparrows, these flying reptiles had long skinny jaws with pointy teeth, probably used for plucking fish from the water. A long tail, like that of a kite, helped to steer them through the air. By 180 million years, the rhamphorynchoids were dispersed worldwide, and suddenly, without explanation, went extinct 150 million years ago.

With the extinction of the rhamphorynchoids, the second evolutionary wave of pterosaurs began. This suborder, called pterodactyloida, was more sizable, and held many differences in appearance. Most notable was the loss of a long tail structure. The jaw became longer, with the loss of teeth that were present in earlier pterosaurs. In addition, the neck became longer, and a large crest began to form on the top of the skull in some species of pterosaurs. The large crests may have grown out to aid as a counterbalance to long jaws, and therefore act as a flight stabilizer. The loss of the tail and development of larger features may indicate a greater intelligence to compensate for difficulties in flight. Detailed analysis of the brain cavity of two pterosaur specimens has indicated the area of the brain that controls flight and eyesight was larger and more developed than even modern day birds. This would signify a greater control of flight while being able to keep eyes focused on prey. This ability became even more important as their size began to push the limits. By the end of their evolution they had reached the upper boundaries of functional size, like their cousins the dinosaurs.

Quetzalcoatlus was the largest example of this. With a 40-foot wingspan, it nearly doubled the size of pteranodon. It is felt by scientists in many fields of research that this is the largest a flying animal could achieve before flight becomes impossible. But despite the ultimate adaptive goals reached, Pterosaurs finally went extinct with all other animals of great size, 65 million years ago.

Returning back to a point in time 85 million years ago, our pteranodon continues to scan the forest and water's edge. From high above he sees one of his evolutionary cousins, a large crocodilian named deniosuchus. Evolved from the thecontians as well, this large crocodilian lay feeding on the remains of some other large and now unidentifiable creature. Measuring over 30 feet in length, it presented a sizable danger to any unwelcome poachers. [12] Pteranodon cautiously stops to circle for any opportunity to partake in this feast. Crocodilians are arguably one of the most successful designs nature has ever created. Representatives of this species can still be found along the Gulf Coast, with seemingly no change in form in over 80 million years. Crocodilians are more closely related to elasmosaurus and other marine reptiles, but still hold the same common ancestor to pterosaurs and dinosaurs.

Not wanting to risk a confrontation with deniosuchus, the Pteranodon moves on in search of other less-guarded carrion. The low tide falls on the Niobraraian Sea, exposing a large dead marine reptile on a beach. Pteranodon is luckily the first to discover it, and quickly descends to feast. The pteranodon glides in low, and with a few mighty flaps of his wings, comes to a stop rising only slightly before landing a safe distance away from the carcass. Standing upright on two legs he scans for danger before proceeding to eat. With his wings tucked inward, he takes several steps forward before dropping on all fours to cover the remaining distance. The pteranodon's pointed jaw is ideal for piercing the soft tissues to extract satisfying portions of meat. As he fills his stomach, small bird-like creatures with the size and appearance of toothy sea gulls begin to arrive on the scene. Despite having similar abilities of flight, they are not related to pteranodon. They are the early ancestors of modern day birds.

The pteranodon is now greatly outnumbered by small sea birds, and several other species of pterosaurs all clamouring for food. Having taken his fill, he walks to the water's edge, and with several large running flaps into the wind he takes flight again. Satisfied with the day's catch, he settles in a small group of other pteranodons floating just off the coast. As the sun sets again, he tucks his jaw under one folded wing and falls fast asleep.

The fictional pteranodon I have portrayed is just one possible scenario based on popular scientific belief. The truth is elusive, and highly debated by palaeontologists across the world. So many pieces of information are missing from the fossil record, that a true picture may be decades away, if ever. In some cases it might take a living, breathing, specimen to answer the question.

Colour is just one aspect of anatomy that may always elude the experts. By looking at the animals of today, we can make only educated guesses about appearance. For example, one such educated guess is that Pteranodon may have had similar colourisation to modern-day sea birds. A white to grey colour on the underside may help to break up a viewable outline against the sky. This would aid the animal to better sneak up on fish just below the surface as well as making them less obvious to the predators beneath the surface. Still other examples are wing attachment points, which may not seem as important but holds the key to locomotion in pterosaurs. The ability to walk upright in some species as suggested by some palaeontologists would be greatly impeded by wings attached to the ankles as opposed to the hip.

Social habits such as nesting in groups have been suggested by fossil evidence of large groupings of young and old pterosaurs, together giving lines of evidence indicating group-nesting behaviour. But further clouding the fossil evidence can be juvenile fossils recovered. A young adult sometimes gives the impression of a *new* find, but later is discovered to belong to a pre-existing species. Eggs have also been discovered in conjunction with these "grouped" fossil beds in different parts of the word. One egg from China exhibits unbelievable preservation, and detailed structures, adding much to the representation of pterosaur development and structure.

Most of the over 100 documented pterosaur species are only known by partial fragments of bones, and vastly incomplete skeletons. In the world of palaeontology, it is very rare indeed to find a completely intact skeleton of any species. Due to the pterosaurs' relationship to water, scientists have had greater success over the past few decades in recovering new species. All bone preservation, relies on the rapid burial of the animal shortly after death. It's not only beneficial to keeping a skeleton intact and away from predators who would scavenge, but to the locking out of oxygen to begin the replacement of bone for rock minerals. The Niobrara Sea was such an ideal environment for fossil preservation. A deep chalk bed deposit left behind by the sea, supplied countless pterosaurs that died at sea. Deposited at its bottom, silts covered the remains of a great many organisms for millions of years.

Countless theoretical changes will no doubt be made over the next century. And misconceptions will be revealed.

Misconceptions regarding the pterosaur family have persisted since the first discovery in 1784. Found in a rock formation that is known for excellent preservation among many different species throughout time, the Solnhofen Limestone is a treasure trove of lost information. Italian naturalist Cosmo Alessando, who stated it was *"an unknown amphibious marine animal of dubious zoological classification",* made the first descriptions.

It was no stretch to place the pterosaurs as early ancestors of birds. Still other theories described them as half-bird and half-bat. In 1801, French Baron Georges Cuvier announced after great study of the fossils that it was a "flying reptile" belonging to a new group of animals. Cuvier stated that "if restored to life, it would resemble nothing in the modern world" and named this fossil "Pterodactlus" or *"Winged finger."* His main logic for the separate lineage, was the radically elongated pinky finger, adapted to support a wing-like structure. This created quite a stir in the scientific community, as well as introducing a new creature of wonder into pop-culture. It is for that reason to this day; most people identify all Pterosaurs as "Pterodactyls."

Since then, numerous new pterosaurs have been discovered, and the lines of ancestry have been moved. Body structures and abilities have been redefined, and debated over and over, with little clarification provided by the fossil record.

Perhaps, just perhaps, the ultimate misconception, and the fantasy of all palaeontologists, is that it never went extinct at all. Perhaps, in some recess of the world a very distant descendent with similar features still exists, waiting to be discovered and provide the answers to all our questions.

Appendix 2

- Chronological Listing of Big Bird Sightings -

1945 - Present – La Palma Colonia, San Benito
Description: many residents claim to have encountered a giant bird with catlike face and no beak, 20' wingspan, big eyes, thick neck, dark feathers with white underside, claws, reportedly makes clicking and whistling sounds and attacks people.

Pre 1958 – Swinney Switch on the Nueces River
Grocery Store Owner from Corpus Christi
Description: creature with fur and feathers that swam beneath the water and then climbed up tree before removing hook and flying away.

1970 – Highway 63 near Welasco
Jesus Martinez
Description: brown bird, as long as a car with a 16' wingspan, head and beak like eagle.

1971 – Harlingen
M. Gonzalez
Description: unusual, brown bird.

October 1975 – Robstown
Witnesses on playground
Description: big, black bird with red markings .

October/November 1975 – Rio Grande City
Description: half human half bird.

Late November 1975 – San Benito
Man and two children
Description: monster bird with bald, monkey-like head.

December 13, 1975 – near Los Fresnos
Description: big bird.

January 01, 1976 – Five miles south of Harlingen along Ed Carey Road
Tracey Lawson & Jackie Davies
Description:" horrible-looking" huge black bird, over 5' tall with wings bunched up at shoulders, which were 3' wide, bald head with gorilla-like grey, face, big dark red eyes, sharp thick beak at least 6" long, made a loud, shrill "eeee" sound, left deep12" tracks.

January 03, 1976 (early morning) – San Benito
Officers Arturo Padilla & Homero Galvan
Description: white bird with 15' wingspan, neck curled up into S shape.

January 07, 1976 (8:30pm) – Tejas Street, just outside of Brownsville
Alverico Guajardo
Description: "something from another planet, like a bird but not a bird," 4' tall with brown feathers, long, bat-like wings folded around its shoulders, "terrifying" red eyes the size of silver dollars, beak 3' to 4' long, throat made horrible pulsing noise .

January 11, 1976 (afternoon) - ranch just north of Poteet
Jesse Garcia & Vanacio Rodriguez.
Description: 5' tall bird that glided as it silently took off.

January 14, 1976 (10:30pm) – north side of Raymondville
Armando Grimaldo
Description: 5'8" tall with wingspan of 10' to 12', blackish-brown, leathery, featherless skin, bat-like or monkey-like face with no beak, bright red 2" to 3" eyes, large claws, made sounds like flapping of bat wings & whistling.

January 14, 1976 – Laredo
Arturo Rodriguez & nephew, Roberto Gonzalez
Description: gigantic, grey bird flying over river and Highway 83.

Mid January 1976 - near a pond several miles northeast of Brownsville
Libby & Deany Ford
Description: man-sized, wings and face like bat, resembled pteranodon.

January 17, 1976 – near Olmito on FM 1575
Unidentified man & family
Description: cat or monkey-faced bird, 4' to 5' tall with 12' wingspan.

January 17, 1976 – irrigation canal at San Benito
Homer & Marie Hernandez
Description: 4' tall bird with 4" to 6" beak.

January 23 - 24, 1976 – Del Rio
Barrera family, V. Castillo, D. Vasquez, J. Kilroy
Description: big, black or bluish grey stork-like bird.

Late 1970s – Brownsville & later Edinburg
Alex Resendez & family
Description: large, brown bird with blue and white stripes under wings, long, transparent-looking beak.

February 24, 1976 (morning) – Southside School District, near San Antonio
Patricia Bryant, Marsha Dahlberg & David Rendon
Description: wingspan of 12' to 20' or more, could see the black skeleton through the background of grey skin or feathers, it just glided no higher than the telephone line, huge breast, peculiar bat-like wings with bony structure and bones at the top and in between, different looking legs, looked like pteranodon.

December 08, 1976 – Montalba
John S. Carroll Jr.
Description: enormous 8' bird, bluish steel-grey with golden-hued breast and 12" bill, weighed about a hundred pounds, had trouble getting airborne.

December 17, 1976 – Bethel
Doloris Moore
Description: very large, like a big crane seen through a magnifying glass, it appeared to have injured wing.

Summer 1981-1983 (6:00pm) – 10005 Lucore Street, Houston
Richard Guzman
Description: leathery bird-like pterodactyl, length about 5' including 2' tail, 5' wingspan, body without feathers, golden tan, brown or beige like leather, bat-like wings, crested head with indentation in the side, pointy beak, long tail ended in diamond shape, mostly glided, flapped its wings a couple of times slowly.

September 14, 1983 (3:55pm) – 4.3 miles east of Los Fresnos along Highway 100
James Thompson
Description: "pterodactyl-like bird," thin body, 8' to 10' in length including tail which terminated in fin, wingspan of 5' to 6', black or greyish rough texture hide-type covering, hump on the back of head, structure near throat like pelican's pouch, no neck, flapped wings just enough to stay above the grass.

1983 (evening) – Hondo
Russell and three other men
Description: giant, feathered bird that blacked out moon.

1990s (evening) – Rangerville
Guadalupe Cantu III & relative
Description: black, with beak like eagle or hawk, 15' wingspan, took off by gliding.

Bibliography

Bord, Janet & Colin – *Alien Animals*
Stackpole Books, Harrisburg, PA 1981

Bord, Janet & Colin – *Unexplained Mysteries of the 20th Century*
Contemporary Books, Chicago, IL 1989

Childress, David Hatcher – *Living Pterodactyls Haunt Our Skies*

Clark, Jerome – *Unexplained!*
Visible Ink Press, Detroit, MI 1993

Clark, Jerome & Coleman, Loren - *Creatures of the Outer Edge*
Warner Books, Inc. 1978

Coleman, Loren – *Curious Encounters*
Faber & Faber, Inc. Winchester, MA 1985

Coleman, Loren & Jerome Clark – *Cryptozoology A to Z*
Fireside Books, New York, NY 1999

Cox, George – *Encounter with Brown Bird Scary Experience*
The Brownsville Herald, TX 1/8/76

Czerkas, Stephen A. & Qiang Ji – *A New Rhamphorhynchoid With A Headcrest and Complex Integumentary Structures* – The Dinosaur Museum, Blanding, UT 2002

Downes, Jon – *The Owlman and Others*
CFZ Publications, Exeter, England 2001

Freeman, Richard – *Dragons: More than a Myth?*
CFZ Publications, Exeter, England 2005

Garcia, Kevin – *El Cucuy Has Roots Deep in Border Folklore*
The Brownsville Herald, TX 10/31/05

Goertzen, John – *The Rhamphorhynchoid Pterosaur Scaphognathus crassirostris: A "Living Fossil" Until the 17th Century*
9/26/98

Gordon, Stan - *Possible Thunderbird Pair Reported in Northeast Pennsylvania*
From the files of Stan Gordon 7/3/02

Gulf Coast Bigfoot Research Organization – *Website (Weird Stuff & Other Cryptids)*
Bobby Hamilton, Warren, TX 2006

Hall, Mark A. – *Thunderbirds: America's Living Legends of Giant Birds*
Paraview Press, New York, NY 2004

Hall, Mark A. – *Wonders, Vol. 10, No.1 The Wings of the Night & No. 2.Flying Dinosaurs*
Mark A. Hall Publications, Wilmington, NC 2006

Hess, Mike – *Big Bird Reported Near San Antonio*
San Antonio Express News 1/15/76

Heuvelmans, Bernard – *On the Track of Unknown Animals*
Hill and Wang, New York 1959

Keel, John A. – *Strange Creatures from Time and Space*
Fawcett Publications, Inc. 1970

Kuban, Glen J. – *"Living Pterodactyls"*

Mackal, Roy P. – *Searching for Hidden Animals*
Cadogan Books, London 1980

McGrath, Jack – *Big-bird trouble may be doubled*
San Antonio Express News 1/14/76

Peterson, Roger Tory – *Field Guide: Birds of Texas and Adjacent States*
The Easton Press, Norwalk, CT 1985

Sanderson, Ivan T. – *Investigating the Unexplained*
Prentice-Hall, Inc. Englewood Cliffs, NJ 1972

Schaffner, Ron – *Recently Obtained Anecdotal Accounts of "Big Birds" and "Pterosaurs"*
North American Biofortean Review #9

Shuker, Karl P.N. – *In Search of Prehistoric Survivors*
Blandford Books, London 1995

Shuker, Karl P.N. – *From Flying Toads to Snakes with Wings*
Llewellyn Publications, St. Paul, Minnesota 1997

Sisk, K. Mack – *Cessna-Sized Big Birds Swoop Over Teachers*
The San Antonio Light 2/26/76

Walzer, Alma – *Feathered Friend? For Some, Legend of Big Bird Remains A Mystery*
McAllen Monitor 10/31/04

Warren, Andy – *Technician Spots 'Mystery Bird'*
Valley Morning Star, Harlingen 2/16/86

Wellenhoffer, Dr. Peter – *The Illustrated Encyclopaedia of Prehistoric Flying Reptiles*
Barnes & Noble Books, New York 1996

Whitcomb, Jonathan – *In Search of the Ropen: Living Pterosaurs of New Guinea*
J. Whitcomb, Paraview Press, Los Angeles 2006

Notes

1. *Wikipedia*: The Big Thicket is the name of a heavily forested area in Southeast Texas. While no exact boundaries exist, the area occupies much of Hardin, Liberty, Tyler, and Polk Counties and is roughly bounded by the Trinity River, Neches River, and Pine Island Bayou. To the north, it blends into the remainder of the larger Piney Woods terrestrial ecoregion of which it is a part.

The Big Thicket has been described as one of the most biodiverse areas in the world. The Big Thicket National Preserve was established in 1974 in an attempt to protect the many plant and animal species within. Big Thicket National Preserve, along with Big Cypress National Preserve in Florida, became the first national preserves in the United States National Park System when both were authorised by the U.S. Congress on October 11, 1974. Big Thicket was also designated as a Biosphere Reserve by UNESCO in 1981. The preserve consists of nine separate land units as well as six water corridors.

2. *Wikipedia:* **Lake Bangweulu** is a large but shallow lake in northern Zambia. It covers a surface area of 5,000 sq km but has an average depth of only 4 m. The lake is part of the Congo River system and is fed by the Chambeshi River from the northeast. The area around Lake Bangweulu is a large wetland known as Bangweulu Swamp or Bangweulu Wetlands. The swamp results from the growth of excessive vegetation, which acts as a check on annual flooding by releasing water slowly through many lagoons and channels. The lake drains into the Luapula River.

The town of Samfya lies on the lake's south western shore, a base for boats to the lake's various inhabited islands. The lake is used by a local fishing industry and is also known for its crocodiles. The missionary David Livingstone died in Chief Chitambo's village on the southern shores of Lake Bangweulu in 1873.

For more information, we refer you to another of our publications: *Fragrant Harbours, Distant Rivers* by J.T.Downes ISO (**ISBN:** 0951287257)

3. Richard Freeman, Zoological Director, CFZ: "This statement from Texas Parks and Wildlife Commission officer Ed Dutch is very strange. To my knowledge the extant species of North American bird with the largest wingspan is the Californian condor *(Gymnogyps californianus*), an incredibly rare bird known from the south-western coastal states. Although they were found in Texas in prehistoric times, they have not been recorded in Texas since records began. Several other species reach a large wingspan: The Atlantic yellow-nosed albatross, (*Thalassarche chlororhynchos*), for example, can attain spans of between 8-9ft, but that seems to be the limit. It would be interesting to know to what species Dutch was referring when he said: *"We have a number of spe-*

cies of birds that do exist in South Texas in the Valley area, many of which have wingspans up to perhaps 10 feet or in excess of 10 feet, and some of them are on the rare endangered species list. All birds are protected by state or federal law, so if any of these birds should be killed or chased or caught for whatever reason it may be they're going to be subject to prosecution by state or federal officials."

4. Jonathan Downes (Director, CFZ): "The world was, indeed, particularly strange during the summer of 1976. One of the strangest places was in the southwest of England, although the events there were mirrored across the world. Although, if you read any of the books on general mystery animals such as *Alien Animals* by Janet and Colin Bord, or indeed any of the contemporary copies of *Fortean Times* the claim that Cornwall had been particularly weird at the time is often made, it is not until you visit the Cornish Studies Library in the back streets of Redruth, sit yourself down at one of their microfiche machines, and physically examine twelve months or more's issues of *The Falmouth Packet*, *The West Briton* and *The Western Morning News* that you can see quite how strange the time actually was. For a period between the late autumn of 1975 and the early spring of 1977 it seems that Southern Cornwall was seized by a period of collective madness. Much of this is chronicled in some depth in my book *The Owlman and Others* but even there I think that I failed to give a true picture of quite how strange the area had become.

There were dramatic extremes in the weather - droughts and floods - heat waves and frozen wastes. The local animal life went (figuratively and literally) crazy; one unfortunate woman was imprisoned in her house by hordes of attacking birds which literally beat themselves to death against the walls of her house, which was dripping red with their blood. Another woman was similarly imprisoned by a mob of feral cats, dog attacks trebled, swimmers were attacked by dolphins (who also saved other swimmers from drowning), and there were reports that cattle belonging to local farmers had developed the power of teleportation. Most interesting to the fortean were the burgeoning numbers of UFO sightings and the reports of three entirely different sets of mystery animal in the region; Morgawr (the Cornish Sea Serpent), the Cornish mystery big cats and the Owlman of Mawnan.

5. Richard Freeman: Recently the fossil remains of an even larger pterosaur have been discovered in Romania:

From the Times of London: 9 Sept. 2005

SKIES THAT WAS BIGGER THAN A SPITFIRE

Mark Henderson, Science Correspondent

A PTEROSAUR with a wingspan almost twice that of the Typhoon Eurofighter is the largest known creature to have flown, scientists said yesterday.

BIG BIRD! - MODERN SIGHTINGS OF FLYING MONSTERS

The flying cousins of the dinosaurs, one of which seized Raquel Welch in the 1966 film One Million Years BC, have long been known to have dwarfed all modern birds. Fossils discovered recently in Mexico, however, suggest that the very largest were even bigger than had been thought possible.

The size of a set of newly identified pterosaur footprints indicates that some of the airborne behemoths had wings that stretched at least 59ft (18m) from tip to tip, and its true dimensions may have been larger still.

Previous estimates had put the biggest pterosaurs, of a species known as Quetzalcoatlus after an Aztec god, at a span of 38ft - as wide as the wings of a Spitfire, but a mere pigeon in comparison with the new beast. Among modern fighter aircraft, the F15's wingspan is 42ft and the Typhoon's 34ft.

Fossilised bones found in Israel, Jordan, Brazil and Romania have also provided evidence of pterosaurs measuring 42ft to 46ft across, suggesting that truly huge individuals may not have been altogether rare.

David Martill, of the University of Portsmouth, a leading authority on pterosaurs, told the BA Science Festival in Dublin that the footprints belonged to the largest flying animal yet discovered.

"Quetzalcoatlus was an animal the size of an aeroplane, with each wing five metres long, but we now have a lot of evidence that these things were even bigger than that," he said. *"The largest may have been nearly twice that size. Experts have come up with estimates that are in excess of 18 metres."*

The fossils were discovered in Mexico by Eberhard "Dino" Frey, of the State Natural History Museum in Karlsruhe, Germany, but details have yet to be published. It is not yet known whether they belong to a new species or a large example of a known one.

Pterosaurs were not dinosaurs, but they lived during the same Triassic, Jurassic and Cretaceous periods from about 220 million years ago to the mass extinction that took place 65 million years ago. The vast flying lizards, of which the most famous are the pterodactyl and the crested pteranodon, lived all over the world.

Dr Martill's research has shed light on how pterosaurs managed to fly, despite their great size. Their secret was a remarkable, almost paper-thin membrane stretched tightly between light, hollow fore and hind limb bones. It gave them highly aerodynamic wings more similar to those of a modern bat than of a bird.

"This membrane was a very, very sophisticated structure," Dr Martill said. *"It was not just a piece of skin. It was a tissue that enabled thermoregulation by acting as a heat exchanger, and was very, very thin - it was not thick and scaly like a crocodile's skin."*

He said that the bone was phenomenally structured, giving very low weight.

Unlike those of modern bats or birds, pterosaur wings were not attached to the upper body but to its lower part, rather as the wings of a jumbo jet protrude from its belly. This would have improved their manoeuvrability, as would the reptiles' joint configuration.

The creatures were probably capable of powered flight and not just gliding, but would have exploited thermal currents in the same way as large, modern birds such as albatrosses and condors. They may have taken off by jumping - their pelvises show structural similarities to those of frogs - and most probably spent most of their lives in the air.

Three fossilised embryos have shown that pterosaur young were born with wings in the same proportions as adults, indicating that they started flying soon after they hatched. Modern birds do not fly until almost fully grown.

Dr Martill said: *"If you were an aviation designer looking at it, you would say how can you build up from the equivalent of a Cessna to a jumbo jet while flying all the time?"* Courtship, he said, would have been conducted "with gusto". Many pterosaurs had crests that would have impaired aerodynamic performance, making it probable that these were used for sexual signalling.

Pterosaurs are known to have been carnivorous, but no stomach contents have ever been discovered. Most species are thought to have eaten mainly fish, though some show adaptations for catching insects and skimming the surface of water for grubs.

Dr Martill said one possible explanation for their vast dimensions is that they simply failed to stop growing at adulthood. *"If they just grew and grew, the oldest individuals would get very large indeed,"* he said. *"It might be quite rare to find these very large ones, as few animals would have lived for the very long periods needed to get that big."*

6. *Wikipedia*: Cameroons was a British Mandate territory in West Africa, now divided between Nigeria and Cameroon.The area of present-day Cameroon was claimed by Germany as a protectorate during the "Scramble for Africa" at the end of the 19th century. During World War I, it was occupied by British, French and Belgian troops, and later mandated to Great Britain and France by the League of Nations in 1922. The French mandate was known as Cameroun and the British territory was administered as two areas, Northern Cameroons and Southern Cameroons.

French Cameroun became independent in January 1960, and Nigeria was slated for independence later that same year, which raised question of what to do with the British territory. After some discussion (which had been going on since 1959), a plebiscite was agreed to, and held in February 1961. The Muslim-majority Northern area opted for union with Nigeria, and the Southern favored Cameroon/Cameroun. Northern Cameroons became a region of Nigeria May 31, 1961, while Southern Cameroons became part of Cameroon on October 1.

7. Jonathan Downes (Director, CFZ): Less well known than Sanderson's ongoing fascination with this animal, which continued -more or less unabated - until the end of his life, was that Gerald Durrell (1925-1995), the spiritual father of the CFZ, was also obsessed with this creature, having been enthused by Sanderson during their long correspondence. Durrell spent a considerable time during his second and third West African expeditions (1949, and 1957) investigating these reports from the Mamfe area. (Source: *Gerald Durrell: The Authorised Biography* by Douglas Botting ISBN: 0006387306

8. *Wikipedia:* Namibia, officially the Republic of Namibia, is a country in southern Africa on the Atlantic coast. It shares borders with Angola, and Zambia to the north, Botswana to the east, and South Africa to the south. It gained independence from South Africa in 1990 and its capital city is Windhoek. Namibia is a member state of the Southern African Development Community (SADC), the African Union (AU), and the Commonwealth of Nations.

The dry lands of Namibia were inhabited since early times by Bushmen, Damara, Namaqua, and since about the fourteenth century AD, by immigrating Bantu who came with the Bantu expansion. The region was not extensively explored by Europeans until the 19th century, when the land came under German control as South-West Africa -- apart from Walvis Bay under British control. South Africa occupied the colony during World War I and administered it as a League of Nations mandate territory until after World War II, when it unilaterally annexed the territory, albeit without international recognition.

In 1966 the Marxist South-West Africa People's Organisation (SWAPO) guerrilla group launched a war of independence, but it was not until 1988 that South Africa agreed to end its administration of Namibia, in accordance with a United Nations peace plan for the entire region. Independence came in 1990, and Walvis Bay was ceded to Namibia in 1994.

9. *Wikipedia*: Prospero Alpini (also known as Prosper Alpinus, Prospero Alpinio and Prosper Alpin) (November 23, 1553 - February 6, 1617), was an Italian physician and botanist.

Born at Marostica, in the republic of Venice, in his youth he served for a time in the Milanese army, but in 1574 he went to study medicine at Padua. After taking his doctor's degree in 1578, he settled as a physician in Campo San Pietro, a small town in the Paduan territory. But his tastes were botanical, and to extend his knowledge of exotic plants he travelled to Egypt in 1580 as physician to George Emo or Hemi, the Venetian consul in Cairo.

In Egypt he spent three years, and from a practice in the management of Date Palms, which he observed in that country, he seems to have deduced the doctrine of the sexual difference of plants, which was adopted as the foundation of the Linnaean taxonomy system. He says that "the female date-trees or palms do not bear fruit unless the branches of the male and female plants are mixed together; or, as is generally done, unless the dust found in the male sheath or male flowers is sprinkled over the female flowers".

On his return, he resided for some time at Genoa as physician to Andrea Doria, and in 1593 he was appointed professor of botany at Padua, where he died on the 6th of February 1617. He was succeeded in the botanical chair by his son Alpino Alpini (d. 1637).

10. *Wikipedia*: The Thunderbird is a mythical creature common to Native American religion. According to the book "Mythological Monsters", its wing span is 3 miles long, and it has a head that grows from its chest.

The thunderbird's name comes from that common supposition that the beating of its enormous wings causes thunder and stirs the wind. The Lakota name for the Thunderbird is "Wakinyan," a word formed from "kinyan," meaning "winged," and "wakan," "sacred." The Kwakiutl called him "Jojo," and the Nootka called him "Kw-Uhnx-Wa." The Ojibwa word for a thunderbird that is closely associated with thunder is "animikii", while large thunderous birds are "binesi." It is described as being two canoe-lengths from wingtip to wingtip, and it creates storms as it flies. Clouds are pulled together by its wingbeats, the sound of thunder is its wings clapping, sheet lightning is the light flashing from its eyes when it blinks, and individual lightning bolts are glowing snakes that it carries with it. In masks, it is depicted as many-colored, with two curling horns, and sometimes with teeth within its beak.

Depending on the people telling the story, the Thunderbird is either a singular entity or a species. In both cases, it is intelligent, powerful, and wrathful. All agree that one should go out of one's way to keep from getting thunderbirds angry.

The singular Thunderbird (as the Nootka believed) was said to reside on the top of a mountain, and was the servant of the Great Spirit. The Thunderbird only flew about to carry messages from one spirit to another.

The plural thunderbirds (as the Kwakiutl and Cowichan tribes believed) could shapeshift to human form by tilting back their beak as if it were only a mask, and by removing their feathers as if it were a feather-covered blanket. There are stories of thunderbirds in human form marrying into human families; some families may trace their lineage to such an event. Families of thunderbirds who kept to themselves but wore human form were said to have lived along the northern tip of Vancouver Island. The story goes that other tribes soon forgot the nature of one of these thunderbird families, and when one tribe tried to take them as slaves the thunderbirds put on their feather blankets and transformed to take vengeance upon their foolish captors.
The Sioux believed that in "old times" the thunderbirds destroyed dangerous reptilian monsters called the Unktehila.

11. *Wikipedia:* Teratorns were very large birds of prey who lived in North and South America from Miocene to Pleistocene. They were somewhat close to modern condors and as such, they are more closely related to storks rather than Accipitridae which includes most other diurnal predatory birds, including Old World vultures; however, Rhys (1980) put the family Teratornithidae in the order Accipitriformes. They include some of the largest known flying birds. So far, four species have been identified:

Teratornis merriami (Miller, 1909). This is by far the best-known species. Over a hundred specimens have been found, mostly from La Brea Tar Pits. It stood about 75 cm (29.5 in) tall with estimated wingspan of perhaps 3.5 to 3.8 metres (11.5 to 12.5 ft), and weighed about 15 kg (33 lbs); making it slightly bigger than extant condors. It became extinct at the end of Pleistocene, some 10,000 years ago. *Teratornis* is Greek for "monster bird".

Aiolornis incredibilis (Howard, 1952), previously known as *Teratornis incredibilis.* This species is fairly poorly known, finds from Nevada and California include several wing bones and part of the beak. They show remarkable similarity with *merriami* but are uniformly about 40% larger: this would translate to wingspan of about 5 metres (16.5 ft) for *incredibilis.* The finds are dated from Pliocene to late Pleistocene which is considerable chronological spread, and thus it is uncertain whether they actually represent the same species.

Cathartornis gracilis (Miller, 1910). This species is known only from a couple of leg bones found from La Brea Ranch. Compared to *T. merriami*, remains are slightly shorter and clearly more slender, indicating more gracile body build.

Argentavis magnificens (Campbell & Tonni, 1980). A partial skeleton of this enormous teratorn was found from La Pampa, Argentina. It is the oldest known teratorn, dating to late Miocene, about 6 to 8 million years ago, and one of the very few teratorn finds in South America. Initial discovery included portions of the skull, incomplete humerus and several other wing bones. Even conservative estimates put its wingspan at 6 metres and up (some 20 ft), and it may have been as much as 8 metres (26 ft). Weight of the bird was estimated to have been around 80 kg (176 lbs). Estimated weight and wing area rival those of the largest pterosaurs.

Another form, *"Teratornis" olsoni*, was described from the Pleistocene of Cuba, but its exact affinities are not completely resolved; it might not be a teratorn at all. There are also undescribed fossils from southwestern Ecuador, but apart from these forms, teratorns were restricted to North America (Campbell & Tonni, 1983).

12. Richard Freeman (Zoological Director, CFZ): "Initial suggestions that this species could reach a length of 50ft were based on over-estimates from fragmentary fossil skulls. It is now known that deniosuchus was an alligator rather than a crocodile, and probably did not get much larger than 30ft. However, other, later species of crocodilian may have attained lengths in excess of 80ft".

Acknowledgments

My sincere thanks and appreciation go out to the following people, without whom this book would not have been possible: My adventurous and beloved wife Lori, as well as our family, `Bam Bamm`, Chester Moore Jr., Kriss Stephens, Bobby Hamilton, Jim Lansdale and the Gulf Coast Bigfoot Research Organization, Jon Downes, Richard Freeman, Nick Redfern and the Centre for Fortean Zoology [CFZ], Scott Marlowe and the Pangaea Institute, Lee Hales, Bill Rebsamen, Richard Guzman, Guadalupe Cantu III, Kevin Garcia and the Brownsville Herald, Lynn David Livsey and the Enlightenment Society, Bill Gibbons, Paul Nation, Jonathan Whitcomb, Phillip O'Donnell, Nick Sucik, John Kirk, Mark A. Hall, Loren Coleman, Jerome Clark and the late, great Dr. Richard Greenwell.

Kenneth James Gerhard was born during a full moon on Friday, October 13th, 1967 in Lansing, Michigan. The son of Canadian immigrants, Ken grew up in Minnesota and Texas, where he developed a love of animals and the outdoors; especially natural mysteries. His interest was encouraged by his mother, who took him to the Amazon in South America, when he was only ten years old. While growing up, Ken's travels included exotic places like Australia's Outback, Thailand, Tunisia, and the Galapagos Islands. He always wanted to learn about the monsters and legendary beasts wherever he went. In 1982 at age fifteen, Ken attempted his first field research, patrolling the shores of Scotland's Loch Ness with a super-8 movie camera. In all, he has traveled to over twenty-five countries on six of the continents and has visited forty-four of the states.

After finishing high school, Ken became involved in music and formed the successful industrial rock bands *Bamboo Crisis* and *Bozo Porno Circus*, as well as the independent Tone Zone Record label. He adapted the stage name Gerhard.

In 2002, Ken rekindled his interest in cryptozoology, and began to investigate various North American cryptids including Wisconsin's Beast of Bray Road, Ohio's Loveland Frog, Ontario's Igopogo and Indiana's Beast of Busco. In September of 2002, he discovered the first of several suspected Bigfoot `nests` in the Big Thicket of East Texas. On subsequent expeditions, Ken has heard and recorded suspected Bigfoot vocalizations, as well as observing eye shine. He has found tracks and other suspected evidence, as well. In all, Ken has searched for Bigfoot in seven different states, and has worked with many respected researchers.

Gerhard has been very active in the search for south Texas' legendary Big Bird, and has uncovered unpublished sightings of that winged monster. In December of 2004, Ken and his wife Lori traveled to the jungles of Belize in order to investigate two unknown hominids known as the Sisemite and Dwendi. The couple found and cast some suspected primate tracks in the Maya Mountains. During July of 2005, Gerhard and paranormal investigator Nick Redfern discovered tantalizing, new evidence of Texas' famous Lake Worth Monster. In November of 2005, Ken helped to lead a state college-backed expedition searching for evidence of Florida's mysterious Skunk Ape.

During January of 2006, Gerhard returned to Belize and led a second expedition to the Maya Mountains. Recently, he was the featured personality on the television program ***Legend Hunters: Bigfoot,*** which aired on Canada's Travel Channel, as well as the History Channel (U.K) during October, 2006. In addition, Ken has appeared on the History Channel's ***Science Meets Legend*** TV series. His credits also include being a guest on the ***Magick Mind Radio*** show, as well as being featured in articles by the ***Orlando Sentinel***, ***Brownsville Herald*** and ***Amarillo Edge,*** as well as websites including ***phenomena.com.***

Ken Gerhard is an active field investigator for ***The Centre for Fortean Zoology,*** as well as the ***Gulf Coast Bigfoot Research Organization***. He has written a self-published book titled ***Monsters are Real***, as well as penning articles for **Animals *and Men***, ***The Journal of the British Columbia Scientific Cryptozoology Club*** and **The *Bigfoot Times***. Ken has lectured twice at the Southern Crypto Conference and also exhibited at paranormal events in Texas and Washington state.

THE CENTRE FOR FORTEAN ZOOLOGY

So, what is the Centre for Fortean Zoology?

We are a non profit-making organisation founded in 1992 with the aim of being a clearing house for information and coordinating research into mystery animals around the world. We also study out of place animals, rare and aberrant animal behaviour, and Zooform Phenomena; – little-understood "things" that appear to be animals, but which are in fact nothing of the sort, and not even alive (at least in the way we understand the term).

Why should I join the Centre for Fortean Zoology?

Not only are we the biggest organisation of our type in the world but - or so we like to think - we are the best. We are certainly the only truly *global* cryptozoological research organisation, and we carry out our investigations using a strictly scientific set of guidelines. We are expanding all the time and looking to recruit new members to help us in our research into mysterious animals and strange creatures across the globe. Why should you join us? Because, if you are genuinely interested in trying to solve the last great mysteries of Mother Nature, there is nobody better than us with whom to do it.

What do I get if I join the Centre for Fortean Zoology?

You get a four-issue subscription to our journal *Animals & Men*. Each issue contains 60 pages packed with news, articles, letters, research papers, field reports, and even a gossip column! The magazine is A5 in format with a full colour cover. You also have access to one of the world's largest collections of resource material dealing with cryptozoology and allied disciplines, and people from the CFZ membership regularly take part in fieldwork and expeditions around the world.

How is the Centre for Fortean Zoology organized?

The CFZ is managed by a three-man board of trustees, with a non-profit making trust registered with HM Government Stamp Office. The board of trustees is supported by a Permanent Directorate of full and part-time staff, and advised by a Consultancy Board of specialists - many of whom who are world-renowned experts in their particular field. We have regional representatives across the UK, the USA, and many other parts of the world, and are affiliated with other organisations whose aims and protocols mirror our own.

I am new to the subject, and although I am interested I have little practical knowledge. I don't want to feel out of my depth. What should I do?

Don't worry. We were *all* beginners once. You'll find that the people at the CFZ are friendly and approachable. We have a thriving forum on the website which is the hub of an ever-growing electronic community. You will soon find your feet. Many members of the CFZ Permanent Directorate started off as ordinary members, and now work full time chasing monsters around the world.

I have an idea for a project which isn't on your website. What do I do?

Write to us, e-mail us, or telephone us. The list of future projects on the website is not exhaustive. If you have a good idea for an investigation, please tell us. We may well be able to help.

How do I go on an expedition?

We are always looking for volunteers to join us. If you see a project that interests you, do not hesitate to get in touch with us. Under certain circumstances we can help provide funding for your trip. If you look on the future projects section of the website, you can see some of the projects that we have pencilled in for the next few years.

In 2003 and 2004 we sent three-man expeditions to Sumatra looking for Orang-Pendek - a semi-legendary bipedal ape. The same three went to Mongolia in 2005. All three members started off merely subscribers to the CFZ magazine.

Next time it could be you!

Project Kerinci, Sumatra - 2003
In search of the bipedal ape Orang Pendek

How is the Centre for Fortean Zoology funded?

We have no magic sources of income. All our funds come from donations, membership fees, works that we do for TV, radio or magazines, and sales of our publications and merchandise. We are always looking for corporate sponsorship, and other sources of revenue. If you have any ideas for fund-raising please let us know. However, unlike other cryptozoological organisations in the past, we do not live in an intellectual ivory tower. We are not afraid to get our hands dirty, and furthermore we are not one of those organisations where the membership have to raise money so that a privileged few can go on expensive foreign trips. Our research teams both in the UK and abroad, consist of a mixture of experienced and inexperienced personnel. We are truly a community, and work on the premise that the benefits of CFZ membership are open to all.

What do you do with the data you gather from your investigations and expeditions?

Reports of our investigations are published on our website as soon as they are available. Preliminary reports are posted within days of the project finishing.

We also publish a 200 page yearbook containing research papers and expedition reports too long to be printed in the journal. We freely circulate our information to anybody who asks for it.

Is the CFZ community purely an electronic one?

No. Each year since 2000 we have held our annual convention - the *Weird Weekend* - in North Devon. It is three days of lectures, workshops, and excursions. But most importantly it is a chance for members of the CFZ to meet each other, and to talk with the members of the permanent directorate in a relaxed and informal setting and preferably with a pint of beer in one hand.

We are hoping to start up some regional groups in both the UK and the US which will have regular meetings, work together on research projects, and maybe have a mini convention of their own.

Since relocating to North Devon in 2005 we have become ever more closely involved with other community organisations, and we hope that this trend will continue. We also work closely with Police Forces across the UK as consultants for animal mutilation cases, and during 2006 we intend to forge closer links with the coastguard and other community services. We want to work closely with those who regularly travel into the Bristol Channel, so that if the recent trend of exotic animal visitors to our coastal waters continues, we can be out there as soon as possible.

Plans are also afoot to found a Visitor's Centre in rural North Devon. This will provide a museum, a library and an educational resource for our members and for researchers across the globe. We are also planning a youth organisation which will involve children and young people in our activities.

Apart from having been the only Fortean Zoological organisation in the world to have consistently published material on all aspects of the subject for over a decade, we have achieved impressive results, including:

- *Disproved the myth relating to the headless so-called sea-serpent carcass of Durgan beach in Cornwall 1975*
- *Disproved the story of the 1988 puma skull of Lustleigh Cleave*
- *Carried out the only in-depth research ever done into mythos of the Cornish Owlman*
- *Made the first records of a tropical species of lamprey*
- *Made the first records of a luminous cave gnat larva in Thailand.*
- *Discovered a possible new species of British mammal - The Beech Marten.*
- *In 1994-6 carried out the first archival fortean zoological survey of Hong Kong.*
- *In the year 2000, CFZ theories where confirmed when an entirely new species of lizard was found resident in Britain.*
- *Proved Existance of giant pike in Llangorse Lake*
- *Confirmed evidence of habitat increase of Armitage's Skink in The Gambia*

Other books available from CFZ PRESS

ONLY FOOLS AND GOATSUCKERS

Jonathan Downes - ISBN 0-9512872-3-0

£12.50

In January and February 1998 Jonathan Downes and Graham Inglis of the Centre for Fortean Zoology spent three and a half weeks in Puerto Rico, Mexico and Florida, accompanied by a film crew from UK Channel 4 TV. Their aim was to make a documentary about the terrifying chupacabra - a vampiric creature that exists somewhere in the grey area between folklore and reality. This remarkable book tells the gripping, sometimes scary, and often hilariously funny story of how the boys from the CFZ did their best to subvert the medium of contemporary TV documentary making and actually do their job.

WHILE THE CAT'S AWAY

Chris Moiser - ISBN: 0-9512872-1-4

£7.99

Over the past thirty years or so there have been numerous sightings of large exotic cats, including black leopards, pumas and lynx, in the South West of England. Former Rhodesian soldier Sam McCall moved to North Devon and became a farmer and pub owner when Rhodesia became Zimbabwe in 1980. Over the years despite many of his pub regulars having seen the "Beast of Exmoor" Sam wasn't at all sure that it existed. Then a series of happenings made him change his mind. Chris Moiser—a zoologist—is well known for his research into the mystery cats of the westcountry. This is his first novel.

CFZ EXPEDITION REPORT 2006 - GAMBIA

ISBN 1905723032

£12.50

In July 2006, The J.T.Downes memorial Gambia Expedition - a six-person team - Chris Moiser, Richard Freeman, Chris Clarke, Oll Lewis, Lisa Dowley and Suzi Marsh went to the Gambia, West Africa. They went in search of a dragon-like creature, known to the natives as `Ninki Nanka`, which has terrorized the tiny African state for generations, and has reportedly killed people as recently as the 1990s. They also went to dig up part of a beach where an amateur naturalist claims to have buried the carcass of a mysterious fifteen foot sea monster named 'Gambo', and they sought to find the Armitage's Skink (Chalcides armitagei) - a tiny lizard first described in 1922 and only rediscovered in 1989. Here, for the first time, is their story.... With an forward by Dr. Karl Shuker and introduction by Jonathan Downes.

BIG CATS IN BRITAIN YEARBOOK 2006

Edited by Mark Fraser - ISBN 978-1905723-01-0

£10.00

Big cats are said to roam the British Isles and Ireland even now as you are sitting and reading this. People from all walks of life encounter these mysterious felines on a daily basis in every nook and cranny of these two countries. Most are jet-black, some are white, some are brown, in fact big cats of every description and colour are seen by some unsuspecting person while on his or her daily business. 'Big Cats in Britain' are the largest and most active group in the British Isles and Ireland This is their first book. It contains a run-down of every known big cat sighting in the UK during 2005, together with essays by various luminaries of the British big cat research community which place the phenomenon into scientific, cultural, and historical perspective.

CFZ PRESS, MYRTLE COTTAGE,
WOOLFARDISWORTHY BIDEFORD,
NORTH DEVON, EX39 5QR
www.cfz.org.uk

Other books available from CFZ PRESS

ANIMALS & MEN - Issues 1 - 5 - In the Beginning
Edited by Jonathan Downes - ISBN 0-9512872-6-5

£12.50

At the beginning of the 21st Century monsters still roam the remote, and sometimes not so remote, corners of our planet. It is our job to search for them. The Centre for Fortean Zoology [CFZ] is the only professional, scientific and full-time organisation in the world dedicated to cryptozoology - the study of unknown animals. Since 1992 the CFZ has carried out an unparalleled programme of research and investigation all over the world. We have carried out expeditions to Sumatra (2003 and 2004), Mongolia (2005), Puerto Rico (1998 and 2004), Mexico (1998), Thailand (2000), Florida (1998), Nevada (1999 and 2003), Texas (2003 and 2004), and Illinois (2004). An introductory essay by Jonathan Downes, notes putting each issue into a historical perspective, and a history of the CFZ.

ANIMALS & MEN - Issues 6 - 10 - The Number of the Beast
Edited by Jonathan Downes - ISBN 978-1-905723-06-5

£12.50

At the beginning of the 21st Century monsters still roam the remote, and sometimes not so remote, corners of our planet. It is our job to search for them. The Centre for Fortean Zoology [CFZ] is the only professional, scientific and full-time organisation in the world dedicated to cryptozoology - the study of unknown animals. Since 1992 the CFZ has carried out an unparalleled programme of research and investigation all over the world. We have carried out expeditions to Sumatra (2003 and 2004), Mongolia (2005), Puerto Rico (1998 and 2004), Mexico (1998), Thailand (2000), Florida (1998), Nevada (1999 and 2003), Texas (2003 and 2004), and Illinois (2004). Preface by Mark North and an introductory essay by Jonathan Downes, notes putting each issue into a historical perspective, and a history of the CFZ.

STRENGTH THROUGH KOI
They saved Hitler's Koi and other stories

£7.99

Jonathan Downes - ISBN 978-1-905723-04-1

Strength through Koi is a book of short stories - some of them true, some of them less so - by noted cryptozoologist and raconteur Jonathan Downes. Very funny in parts, this book is highly recommended for anyone with even a passing interest in aquaculture.

CFZ PRESS, MYRTLE COTTAGE,
WOOLFARDISWORTHY BIDEFORD,
NORTH DEVON, EX39 5QR
www.cfz.org.uk

Printed in the United Kingdom
by Lightning Source UK Ltd.
119535UK00001B/373-378

9 781905 723089